Clearing Life's Hurdles

Dan Baumann

Regal Books
A Division of GL Publications
Ventura, CA U.S.A.

The translation of all Regal books is under the direction of GLINT. GLINT provides technical help for the adaptation, translation and publishing of books for millions of people worldwide. For information regarding translation contact: GLINT, P.O. Box 6688, Ventura, California 93006.

Published by Regal Books
A Division of GL Publications
Ventura, California 93006
Printed in U.S.A.

Library of Congress Cataloging in Publication Data

Baumann, Dan.
    Clearing life's hurdles.

    Includes bibliographical references.
    1. Christian life—1960-   I. Title.
BV501.2.B384528   1984   248.8'4   83-21238
ISBN 0-8307-0926-6

To Stan and Elaine Quade,
Dear Friends
Who have helped us cope.

CONTENTS

*A Teacher's Manual and Student Discovery Guide for Bible
study groups using this book are available from your church
supplier.*

One

The Unknown

We begin with two presuppositions. The first is this: *Everybody faces crisis and change; nobody is immune.*

Dr. Thomas Holmes of the University of Washington concludes that there are at least forty-three areas where you and I have to learn to manage change and crisis to stay healthy. If we don't cope, we are subject to problems. He gives impact points to each of these crises—forty-three of them. He says if you get two hundred impact points in one year, you are a high risk for either physical or mental breakdown. If you have two hundred points in any twelve-month period, you are subject to a major breakdown.[1]

Let me give you some of these (you may want to add up your points): The death of a spouse is 100 impact units. (That is the greatest crisis that Holmes isolated in the study.) The second is divorce—73 units. The death of a family member is 63; marriage is 50; being fired from work is 47;

retirement is 45; pregnancy is 40; change in financial status is 38; son or daughter leaving home is 29. (I have known people who have gone through this one, and it was almost like a divorce when their children left. They were destroyed by it.) Trouble with in-laws is 29; outstanding personal achievement is 28. (If you get an award at work you are in for some impact units. Most valuable player on a ball club will have problems dealing with that. Success can be a very difficult thing to cope with.) Beginning or ending of school is 26; change in residence—20; change in school—20; change in eating habits is 15; Christmas you get 12; 11 if you get a traffic ticket. All he is saying is that all of these changes, these crises, these things that occur to us have an impact on us. Put them all together, and they can become very critical. Everybody faces crisis.

The second presupposition is that *everybody must learn to cope with crisis and change.* If you don't, you become crippled, maimed, and shelved emotionally, socially, or spiritually. But if you learn to cope and learn to manage, you move on to become more mature, more understanding, more enriched—better capable of serving God.

Let me define what it means to cope. The *Oxford Dictionary* has a huge section devoted to coping, and it uses such strong words as "come to blows with," "fight with," "encounter," "prove oneself a match for," "engage in." Those are definitions of cope. Let me give you mine (taken from *Random House Dictionary*): "struggle or contend with some degree of success"—and I would add, "in Christ." To cope is to struggle or contend with some degree of success in Christ.

Our first subject is "Coping with the unknown." How do you deal with the unknown? How do you deal with what is mysterious and still ahead? How do you deal with anything that does not yet have definition? How do you deal with what is hazy and distant and uncertain? Most of us are comfortable with the familiar but fearful of the unknown.

A young person, for example, starts school or transfers to a new school. Friends of ours just moved to the Los Angeles area. Their high school daughter started school, and the first day the teacher looked up and said, "Oh, no, another student!" That kind of attitude doesn't help a student to cope, nor was the faculty member coping. Change—new faces, new situations, new environment.

Or maybe you have a new job and you wonder if you have replaced somebody the other employees liked. You knew your old job well and had been at it for years, but now, all of a sudden, everything is new and uncertain.

Or you move into a new home. In the old house, when you drove home, you knew to turn at the third tree. You backed out of the garage and you swerved around that bush. At night when the lights were out you knew every switch in the house. You could make your way through every room because you knew the floor plan, the furniture, its placement—everything was so familiar. But now you have a new house. Where did they put the switches in this place?

All of a sudden you leave the security blanket of school and go to work full time. Or—even more shattering—after working all your life, suddenly mandatory retirement comes. How do you deal with that? Or your job becomes obsolete and no longer exists. You have to learn to live with this change that is not of your choice and not because of your age. But the job is gone. How do you deal with change?

The reason change is so fearful to us is that we keep reading horror stories and identify with them. A recent newspaper article told about a couple—a mother, sixty-three, and her middle-aged son—who for 448 days had been living in a rusted-out car. When I read that story I thought, "How many people are going to identify with this?" Her husband had been an accountant, and the family lived in La Jolla, California. The son was making $45,000 a year at Chrysler Corporation. Then all of a sudden the husband died, they lost their home in La Jolla, the son lost his job with Chrysler. For 448 days they had been living in a rusted-out car—he slept in the front seat, she in the back. They went to public places to shower and change clothes, and they had to keep moving because it was illegal to sleep in a car. We read such stories and see people who had everything. What right do we have to assume that our future is bright when we hear stories of failure, of people who, two years short of retirement, were cut off from their jobs and denied retirement privileges? We look at such stories and say, "What if it were me?"

As Clyde Narramore, the psychologist, has noted, we look at tomorrow through the eyeglasses of yesterday. If yesterday we had trouble and uncertainty and heartache, we look through that prism into tomorrow—and we assume that tomorrow is simply an extension of yesterday's problems.[2] We fear it. How do you deal with that?

Israel had come out of Egypt. The people were on their way to the Promised Land, but now they were in the wilderness in between. They were uncertain of the future. They looked into tomorrow and saw an imperfect and obscure definition. They looked ahead and did not understand, so they were afraid. Moses gathered them together; it was time for a sermon. In Deuteronomy 11 we read the story of God's man giving God's word to God's people as they coped with the unknown of tomorrow.

Affirm the Known

The first thing he did was to remind them of how good God is. Remember "the Lord your God: his majesty, his mighty hand, his outstretched arm; the signs he performed and the things he did in the heart of Egypt, both to Pharaoh king of Egypt and to his whole country; what he did to the Egyptian army, to its horses and chariots, how he overwhelmed them with the waters of the Red Sea as they were pursuing you, and how the Lord brought lasting ruin on them" (Deut. 11:2-4). He did all that! "Israel, do you remember that you left Egypt? Do you remember when you had the Egyptian army behind you and the Red Sea in front of you and God opened up the waters for you? God dealt with the Egyptian army. God fed you manna and gave you water to drink. God led you and brought you to this place. That is the God you know. Affirm that. Claim that. It's your history."

How do *you* deal with tomorrow? Claim the

God you have known. He is good and He cares and He is trustworthy.

What do we know about God? As we gather like the people of Israel before our uncertain future, what do we have to say? We can say that God has been good. We have experienced redemption. We have experienced the love and the care of the Body of Christ. We have experienced a large measure of health and prosperity and so much more. That is our story.

A Russian immigrant had a toothache and went to a dentist. The American dentist extracted his tooth, and the Russian asked, "What does that cost?" The dentist said, "Fifty dollars for the extraction." The Russian was pleased. "That is reasonable, that is cheap enough." He paid the $50 and said, "In Russia we pay $150 for that." The dentist said, "That is exorbitant." And the Russian said, "Yes, and it is very difficult—a very tough job, because in Russia we cannot open our mouths." One of the things that we in America take for granted is our freedom. We are blessed with so much that is good and available and plentiful. I have a friend who said, "Anybody can succeed in America. Not many do, but that is because not many want to. Anybody can succeed triumphantly." Whether that is right or wrong, there is potential, there is opportunity because we have freedom. We have so much.

The second thing you need to know is that God knows you. And His goodness is personalized—He knows you by name. The personalization of God's providential care is written all across the pages of Holy Scripture. He knows us, and He knows us by name. He goes before His sheep and calls even them by name.

One day my dad came home and he was ecstatic! He had been to a dinner where Billy Graham was the guest of honor. After dinner my dad stood in a reception line with 300 to 400 people. When Dad stuck out his hand Billy Graham said, "Hi, Roy. How have you been?" My dad lived off that for years. A long time earlier Billy Graham had purchased a radio from my dad in his little radio shop, and Dr. Graham never forgot him. "He knows me by name." There is something about being known by name. When God knows you, that is far better than if anybody else knows you. He is a God of grace and goodness, and He is a God who personalizes it when He knows you by name.

The third thing is that God does not change. In Hebrews 13 we read that Jesus Christ is the same yesterday, today, and forever. If any of you has gone back to a reunion, one of the things that struck you is that some of the folks you went to school with twenty-five or so years ago have changed. They were quiet once, and now they are aggressive, used-car-salesmen types. Or maybe they were leaders in your class, but today they are quiet people. If they weren't wearing name tags you wouldn't know them. People change—sometimes radically; but the God of Israel, the God of the early Church, the God of 1984 is the God of eternity future. You build on His unchangeableness. He *is good* and He *knows you* and He *won't change.*

"I am your history!" That is what Moses told Israel; that is what the Word of God tells the people of God. Remember Him! He is the God of tomorrow!

Learn from Yesterday

Deuteronomy 11 contains an interesting verse—verse 6—that has a certain horror to it. "What he did to Dathan and Abiram, sons of Eliab the Reubenite, when the earth opened its mouth right in the middle of all Israel and swallowed them up with their households, their tents and every living thing that belonged to them." In Numbers 16 we discover that these two men had come to Moses and Aaron and complained. They were not happy with what was going on. They were dissatisfied with the things that had occurred to Israel, and they began to complain. Moses said, "Well, bring it before God and let Him deal with it." They refused. Then God told the people, "Step back from these two and their families; clear the way; back up." They all backed up, and the earth opened and swallowed up those two men, their wives, their children, their animals, their whole families and all that they owned. There wasn't much complaining in Israel for a few days! It is a bit like going by a terrible automobile accident— you begin to drive much more carefully.

What Moses was saying to Israel is this: Learn from failure and from yesterday. Don't go back and do the same foolish things again. Learn from experience and let God take you to the next step. One of our songs puts it like this: "Each victory will help you another to win." As you face tomorrow you build it on the blocks of lessons learned today and yesterday. Don't go back and do the same things again. Ask for forgiveness and move on.

Four and a half years ago things had been building and I was beginning to feel like a steam engine about ready to explode. One day I became very angry. Rather than say a word, I went into my office and slammed the door. The place became deathly silent, except for a wall plaque that fell to the floor. It fell behind a four-drawer file, and the file was filled with papers. I had to get out a little hand dolly and slide it underneath the file case to pull it away from the wall. I picked up the plaque to return it to its place, and read it: "Lord, help me to be slow—slow to anger." Very sheepishly I put my plaque back on the wall, went out, brought my staff together, and apologized like a whipped puppy. I have not slammed a door in four and a half years. I trust that I won't slam any more doors. Lord, help me not to do those dumb things but to learn from them and to build on yesterday's lessons.

Sometimes these lessons are so painfully graphic, but you build on them and say, "Learn from yesterday. It's good training for tomorrow."

Anticipate the Unexpected

"The land you are entering to take over is not like the land of Egypt, from which you have come, where you planted your seed and irrigated it by foot as in a vegetable garden" (Deut. 11:10). For years the Israelites had been in Egypt, a place with very little vegetation. Fly over Egypt even today and you will discover a long slender green patch cutting through the desert. In the midst of the green is the meandering Nile River. The Egyptians irrigate just the land that flanks the river into the delta. Apart from the delta and the irrigated areas, Egypt is bleak and without vegetation.

When God's people were in Egypt they dug ditches and irrigated the land by foot to grow their crops. Moses is telling them that was the way it was in Egypt; but it is not going to be like that in Israel. "Israel is rocky and has hills and mountains. Israel has rain and vegetation. You don't know what is ahead of you, but it is different. You may anticipate that tomorrow will not be identical to today." Anticipate realistically that tomorrow brings change.

Some change is good. The British preacher Leonard Griffith, in one of his sermons, tells of visiting a play yard with his grandchild where there were a number of rides for children. He watched the locomotive driver operate a little train. It meandered around little curves and blew an eerie whistle. The engineer was a bit large for that small locomotive. Essentially, he was stuffed into it. Griffith said, "I have never seen such a bored man in all my life." He would get in, start, navigate those turns, push that eerie whistle, stop, let the kids out, get the kids in, start, navigate those turns, push that eerie whistle—all day long. Griffith points out that it is a parable on life.[3] Many people seemingly are caught up in the monotony of sameness. Change is good. We need it. And sometimes we don't have to invite it, it simply comes.

Dr. Richard Chase, formerly at BIOLA and now the new president of Wheaton College, helped me recently. I was wondering whether to consider the possibility of becoming pastor of College Avenue Baptist Church in San Diego, and so I met with him. In our conversation he said, "I have been here at BIOLA eleven years. It is time to change. It is good to change. People may not understand it, but we need it. Change is good for us, good for the school, good for me." And he changed. Some change adds a certain zest and challenge to life which we need.

Change, however, can be painful. Recently a friend of mine, Bob Coates, went in for a routine physical examination. The doctors found a shadow on an x-ray. Surgeons operated and removed some cancer. They thought they had gotten it all. Then two or three weeks later, Bob went back in for eight hours of surgery to remove cancer that had worked its way through his lymph glands. Bob is a big, healthy, husky guy—but we don't know about our tomorrows, do we?

Although change is sometimes painful, God can be trusted with our change. Do you remember when Paul had the thorn in the flesh? I don't know what it was. Some have guessed it was epilepsy—I think that is unlikely. Others feel it was eye trouble—I think that is more likely. Whatever it was, in the midst of that pain Paul wrestled. In three extended periods of his life he asked God to change the situation, but He didn't. God provided two things for him: A friend called Luke, and a lesson: "My grace is sufficient" (2 Cor. 12:8). Into the unexpected comes the assurance that regardless of what it is, God in His grace will be sufficient.

Trust Him and Serve Him

"If you faithfully obey the commands I am giving you today—to love the Lord your God and to serve him with all your heart and with all your soul—Then I will send rain on your land in its season, both autumn and spring rains, so that you may gather in your grain, new wine and oil. I will provide grass in the fields for your cattle, and you will eat and be satisfied" (Deut. 11:13-15). He is saying, "Seek me and my will, and all these things will be cared for." Those who have learned to commit their way, to trust Him and to serve Him, move into tomorrow linked up with the resources and the strength of the God they serve. The text does not say anything about their feelings. People in Hebrews 11 were great heroes of faith who went out sometimes contrary to the evidence, and the only thing they knew is that God was worthy of their trust. They trusted Him.

I don't know what is in your tomorrow. I don't have any idea what is in my tomorrow. But you and I both know that the God who sees all of our tomorrows in a single glance knows all of us by name. He says, "My grace is sufficient. Trust me."

For Further Thought

1. Is there anything about your future that is fearful? Why do you think that is so? What positive steps can you take to alleviate that anxiety?

2. What do you know about God's dealing in your past that gives you confidence regarding the future?

3. Can you turn over your future to God for safekeeping? Why not try it right now?

Notes
1. Lloyd H. Ahlem, *Living with Stress* (Ventura, CA: Regal Books, 1978), pp. 19-21.
2. Clyde M. Narramore, *How You Can Have a Piece of Tomorrow* (Rosemead, CA: Narramore Foundation), p. 4.
3. A. Leonard Griffith, "Land of Beginning Again," *Pulpit Digest*, December 1966, pp. 41-42.

Two

Temptation

In 1 Corinthians 10:11-13, the Apostle Paul is rehearsing warnings out of Israel's history. He is reminding them of lessons learned, lessons that arose out of failure: "These things happened to them as examples and were written down as warnings for us, on whom the fulfillment of the ages has come. So, if you think you are standing firm, be careful that you don't fall! No temptation has seized you except what is common to man. And God is faithful; he will not let you be tempted beyond what you can bear. But when you are tempted, he will also provide a way out so that you can stand up under it."

A number of years ago the city of Chicago had a large billboard that flashed its message across the whole downtown area. Driving along the expressway you could see those large letters leaping out at you: "The best way to overcome temptation is to yield."

God has a better idea. The text before us

reminds us that God's way is the way of victory. The words *tempt* and *temptation* usually mean something rather sinister, as if we were dealing with sin. To be sure, that is the negative side of temptation; but biblically *to tempt* also has a positive side: "to put to the test," "to prove," "to test metal." That's the reason why we read in the Word of God the following: "Consider it pure joy . . . whenever you face trials" (Jas. 1:2). The verbs translated "to tempt" can also be translated "to test." They have the potential for holiness as well as for sin—for proving character or for inducing us to sin.

Temptation needs to be looked at as a conflict that goes on between Christ the Creator and Satan the destroyer. What God does He does well. What Satan does is to destroy the works of God. In Genesis 1 and 2 we have God the Father, God the Son, and God the Holy Spirit in creation, bringing about that which was good. At the end of each day God said, "It is good." When everything was finished God looked on all that He had made and He said, "It is very good." God creates and He does it well. In Genesis 3 Satan then came to destroy the work of God. He took that which had been created and sought to erode it and destroy it.

That is the conflict that goes on in the world. It goes on in our neighborhoods. It goes on in your home and my home, and it goes on in the human heart. The conflict that goes on in your life and in mine is between the work of God, which is to create, and the work of Satan which is to destroy.

Temptation Is Inevitable
The text first of all reminds us that temptation

is inevitable. You might say, "I didn't need a text to tell me that." Temptation has "seized" you, and that is a strong word. It is the picture of something grabbing you and holding you tight in its vise-like grip. Have you been there? Have you felt that? When you are dealing with temptation in your life and it has a stranglehold on you, you know what that's like. But such temptation is common to man. Don't think that you are the only one who has been down that trail, because many have walked it before you. Don't think you are the only one who has fought that battle, because many others have struggled. Don't think you are the only one who has ever experienced temptation, because thousands across 1,900 years of Church history have also done so. We are the community of the tempted. If I understand Hebrews correctly, Jesus also was tempted just as we are. Temptation is common to us. It is human to be tempted.

First John 2:16 gives us a typology of temptation. It does not exhaust the word *temptation* but gives us insight into its nature. "For everything in the world—the cravings of sinful man, the lust of his eyes and the boasting of what he has and does—comes not from the Father but from the world." As the King James Version puts it, we are tempted by "the lust of the flesh, and the lust of the eyes, and the pride of life." If you look into the life of our Saviour, you will discover that all three elements were there in His temptation in Luke 4.

The first temptation—"take this stone and turn it into bread"—is the lust of the flesh, the appeal to the senses. Secondly, Satan takes Him to a high place and says, "Look at all this; look at all you can see. I will give it to you if you will bow down before me." That's lust of the eyes. "You can have that!" Finally, he tempts Him a third time—"Jump off and let your angels care for you"—the pride of who you are. These three temptations are cravings of the senses, the lure of things, and the pride of life.

The cravings of the senses

The temptation is to look at the lust of the flesh, or the cravings of the senses, as if it is limited to sexual sin—and certainly that is included. One modern version *(TLB)* translates the phrase as "the craze for sex." But the cravings of the senses also include gluttony, being enslaved to pleasure, lusting after possessions—anything that appeals to our senses so that we are led by our drives instead of controlling them.

The lure of things

The second category that John talks about—the lust of the eye, or the lure of things—is anything that bombards us from without so that we become insatiably caught up with wanting and desiring something and going after it until it is ours. It is the approach to life that looks on the whole world as a shopping spree. It is to listen to the raucous voice of Madison Avenue and hear that you deserve this car because you've earned it, and so you begin to go after it. It is to heed the commercial on the housing area that says this is where you must live, this is the only place in life that is worthy of your position, and you buy into that and go after it. Or you see a dress and you say, "I have got to have that dress." I have known people like that, and all they talk about is what they have, what they are getting and what they are after. It's the lust of the eye. Life is one big shopping window, and they want it. When we hear a child say, "Gimme, gimme, gimme," we say, "Naughty boy." And then Mommy says it with a little more sophistication: "I need that." But the principle is the same: It is the lure of things.

The pride of life

As the text puts it, " . . . boasting of what he has and does—comes not from the Father but from the world" (1 John 2:16). John uses an interesting word here, a word that suggests receiving a great blessing or achieving something great, something that is very satisfying, and claiming it as our own when we do not deserve it. For example, you boast of your great talent and then you discover that God gave it to you; or you are proud of your looks but you really had very little to do with them because basically God gave them to you. It is to be proud of what we have really not earned.

Recently some of the men of our church challenged the staff to a softball game. It turned out to be one of the low moments in church history. Outside of one or two of our staff members, it looked as if we had been spending a great deal of time in our offices. The folks from the congregation "cleaned our clocks." They gave us six outs as we moved along in some of the innings to encourage our hearts, and even that didn't do it. After that kind of experience, pride is not a big problem. In fact, you usually take your phone off the hook and try to avoid people.

But when you do something noteworthy, then you are in for trouble. When did Jesus receive the three great temptations in the desert? Right after the blessing of His baptism. When did Elijah have his great problem? Right after the conquest of the prophets of Baal in Mount Carmel. When did Israel become defeated by a little town called Ai? After they had conquered the great city of Jericho. When did Peter go through his great trial and fail? Right after he had come from the upper room, from the garden, from a prayer meeting with his Lord. When you are on the mountaintop, then comes the test of pride. When you are doing well, then comes the temptation to say, "Aren't we doing well?" That's why Paul in 1 Corinthians 10, precedes verse 13 with verse 12: "So, if you think you are standing firm, be careful that you don't fall!" Self-deception in pride can topple you in the midst of doing well.

God Is Faithful

The second great theme that comes from the text is that God is faithful. He will not let you be tempted beyond what you can bear. God is worthy of our total reliance. He is never faithless but always proves faithful. He stands behind His promise. Regardless of what you go through—test, trial, temptation—mark it well: He is faithful. "He will not let you be tempted beyond what you can bear" (1 Cor. 10:13).

This means that *He does permit temptation,* and people go through times that I don't understand. Some folks have gone through deep, deep waters and God has allowed it. I don't know why some people have had such great problems with their children. I don't understand why some people have gone through such great difficulties financially, but they have. I don't understand why God allows such things to happen, but I do know that God does not tempt. James 1:13 says that God does not "tempt anyone."

The next truth I understand a little better: *God regulates.* He will not allow you to be tempted beyond certain boundaries that you can handle. Job is the object of conversation between God and Satan. Satan says, "I can't get to him." God says to Satan, "You can do what you choose, but don't take his life. That is where I draw the line" (see Job 1:6-12). There are parameters and fences established by God. You are tempted only up to a certain point—not more than you can bear. When we fail it is not because the temptations are too great; it is because we have not claimed the power available to us. God assists us. God is for us; He is not our adversary—He is our Friend. He is not our enemy—He is the one who stands with us. He is the Faithful One—God is faithful.

Victory Is Possible

That last phrase reminds us of our text's third great theme: Victory is possible. "When you are tempted, he will also provide a way out so that you can stand up under it" (1 Cor. 10:13). Here we see a picture of an army with its back to a mountain. It is about to be defeated as the enemy attacks. Suddenly, in the midst of a bleak situation that seemingly has no promise, the army sees a pass through the mountain and makes its escape. In much the same way, when you come to those times that look so bleak, so dark, so hopeless, God provides a tunnel through which you may escape to victory and not defeat.

Here are five *R*s—biblical encouragements for victory. They don't exhaust all that the Bible has to say, but they give us some clues as to how God provides tunnels for us.

The first *R* is *replace*. We read in Romans 12:21, "Overcome evil with good." Replace whatever puts great stress and tension on you with something that does not. For example, if any of you has been caught up in the drug culture, those who have worked with people on drugs say, "If you are serious about changing, don't go to rock concerts. They are very difficult for people struggling with drugs." So you replace the rock concerts with another form of music or another endeavor. You replace what for you has become evil with something that becomes good.

Second, *resist*. "Resist the devil, and he will flee from you" (Jas. 4:7). At the conclusion of our Lord's three temptations He says, "Satan, be gone." "Satan, beat it." It is a command. He looks Satan in the face and challenges him and resists him and says, "Be gone." In the same way, when you face temptation you must call Satan by name and resist him.

Third, *run*. Paul writes to young Timothy and says, "Flee the evil desires of youth" (2 Tim. 2:22). The word *youth* here applies much more broadly than simply to a teenager. When Joseph was enticed by Potiphar's wife it was not the time for him to discuss patriarchal morality. It was not the time to sit down and say, "Our God tells us to be holy." It was the time to RUN. When a young man and a young woman are in a car and it is late at night and their feelings are warming up and their automatic pilot has gone on, it is not the time to discuss the college-age Sunday School class; it is time to unlock the door and get out and go back to the dorm room. There are times when there is nothing to be said; there is only something that must be done—and that is to run.

Fourth *recall.* In Luke 4, each of our Lord's three temptations is concluded with this phrase: "It is written." In each instance the Lord Jesus claims the authority and the power of the Word of God. Satan himself had quoted Scripture, but not in context. Jesus, however, properly applies the Word of God in its fulness: "It is written." The psalmist wrote, "I have hidden your word in my heart that I might not sin against you" (Ps. 119:11). The Word of God becomes part of your ammunition against temptation. It gives the Spirit of God something to use in your life. Hide it away in your life. Memorize it. Study it. It is artillery for conflict.

Finally, *reach out.* Claim your resources. Claim what is yours. Peter failed His Lord three times for a couple of reasons. First, he was afraid. He was fearful for his life. He thought that he might join the Lord and go the way of the cross. But there was a second problem: Peter failed because he was alone. Can you imagine Peter denying his Lord three times if he had been there with James and John? Can you imagine Elijah having his problem with depression if he had been surrounded by some of the seven thousand that had not bowed the knee, if they had been there for prayerful support and encouragement? (See 1 Kings 19:14-18.) Our biggest problems arise when we are alone. Alcoholics Anonymous knows that lesson. They say, "When you are tempted, call somebody else who is also fighting that battle. They understand, they will stand with you."

Reach out and claim your resources in the Body of Christ. Reach out and claim who Christ Himself is. Hebrews tells us that He was tempted in all points just as we are, yet without sin. Therefore He is able to help, to aid, to strengthen, to enable us. He stands there to assist. He knows what you are going through, and He wants to help. Reach out and claim that promise.

G. A. Studdert-Kennedy in one of his sermons says, "Temptation is not sin. Being attacked is not being defeated; and God can and will deliver us from evil. Only *we must stick to God.* We must rise from our knees and go out into the world, but we must not go out into the world without rising from our knees."[1] The alcoholic says, "I'm not sure about tomorrow, but today I am going to be dry." The Christian says, "I don't know about tomorrow, but today I am going to be victorious over temptation, so help me, God! I'm going to claim that!" No temptation has "seized" you, but such as all of us have known about. Our God is faithful, and He will not allow you to be tempted beyond what you and I can handle, but He will provide a tunnel that we may be able to escape. Victory is available. Would you claim that?

For Further Thought

1. In what area of your life is temptation the biggest problem?

2. What is implied in the statement that "God is faithful"?

3. What can you do immediately to successfully cope with an ongoing temptation in your life?

Note
1. "Lead Us Not Into Temptation" *20 Centuries of Great Preaching*, Clyde E. Hunt, Jr. and William M. Pinson, Jr., eds. (Waco, Texas: Word Books Publishers, 1971), p. 261.

Three

Success

We often have trouble handling our successes. Success is always a crisis and is sometimes handled very poorly.

In our first chapter we referred to Dr. Thomas Holmes who had done a study and concluded that there were at least forty-three major crises that people go through. Each one impacts our life and gives us a jolt (some more than others). Most impactful is the death of a spouse (100 impact units). Number forty-three, at the bottom of Holmes's list, is a minor violation of the law (11 impact units). In twenty-fifth place (28 impact units) is an outstanding personal achievement. Holmes is saying that when you succeed, it's a crisis. When you achieve success in your life—whether academic or athletic or social or monetary—it always comes as a shock to your system. How do you handle that? What do you do?

The Problems of Success

All of us have one type of success or another during our life. What are the symptoms? What are the problems? I would like to suggest at least four.

Demands

The minute you succeed, the expectations that people have of you become greater. If you get an *A* in calculus, your classmates begin to ask questions and seek you out between classes. All of a sudden you are the resident calculus authority. You make the ball team and become "the most valuable player," and everybody begins to look up to you. It's easier to get dates. All kinds of good things happen. But the demands also become higher. When you play a good game, they expect you to play a better game. When you succeed in the business world, all of a sudden people think you are an authority. You earn lots of money, and suddenly everybody knocks on your door.

I knew a man who worked as a $10,000-a-year engineer. He was a happy, quiet, gracious Christian gentleman. His company offered its stock at a dollar per share. The man brought together all of his savings from across the years—$5,000—and bought five thousand shares. Then he went out and borrowed another $5,000 from the bank and bought another five thousand shares. He now owned ten thousand shares of a little company called Control Data. Those shares went up and split, went up and split again, went up and split again. Ten thousand dollars of commitment soon were worth two and one-half to three million dollars.

All of a sudden my Christian friend had people

knocking on his door. They made him chairman of committees; they gave him all kinds of privileges and responsibilities. One day when we were chatting he said, "I have been placed in positions I know nothing about simply because I succeeded in one area. They think I am an authority in every area." The demands on you go up when you succeed, and it really doesn't matter what the area is. All of a sudden the expectations people have of you go up.

Detachment

When people suddenly succeed, their relationships with people and with God begin to deteriorate. I have seen people who walked with God and were faithful to Him and to His people. Then they had a modicum of success, and all of a sudden they became very independent and began to detach themselves from their old friends who were not worthy of their new position. Soon they also began to walk independently of God and the people of God as if they no longer needed Him or His people. That is one of the tragedies that often attends success in our kind of world. The devil uses it as a wedge to separate us from the people who need us and whom we need and from our Lord whom we need.

A gentleman in Chicago—a faithful churchman, a leader in his congregation, a Sunday School teacher—worked as a salesman and did fairly well across the years. He was an outstanding man with a fine family. And then he bought his own business. It began to expand and grow. He soon dropped his Sunday School teaching, resigned from the church board, and left some of his old friends because they didn't run as he ran. They were moving to a different drumbeat. He stopped attending church for years. Somehow he felt that now that he had achieved, now that he had success, he no longer needed people, friends, God. The devil used success as a wedge in his life.

Maybe that is why the Lord Jesus said, "It is hard for a rich man to enter the Kingdom of God." Sometimes the rich become dependent on their riches and become independent of everything else. They feel, "What do I need? I can have it. I can buy it. I can possess it." Position, resources, opportunities—whatever it is, it sometimes destroys those relationships and friendships with people and our Lord that are so important in our lives.

Dethronement

Ahab, the weak king, goes back to his wife, the strong queen Jezebel, and reports to her all that has happened. He says that Elijah killed all of her prophets, and she is incensed: "May the gods deal with me, be it ever so severely, if by this time tomorrow I do not make [Elijah's] life like that of one of them" (1 Kings 19:2). "I want him dead," she is saying. "He may be on the mountaintop today, but I want him dethroned. I don't want him there."

There is a perversity in human nature that asks when people succeed, "How did they do it? They must have cheated. They must have taken advantage. They must have been unethical. They must have inherited it all." Somehow we find it very difficult to rejoice with those who rejoice. It is much easier to weep with those who weep. We see success in another and we wonder, "How did he do it?" We want to dethrone them.

My son joined me at a holiday basketball tournament some years ago, and we had seats so high up that we were both nursing a nosebleed. We said to one of the ushers, "Look at all those seats down there behind the basket. Could we go down there?" He said, "Yes, you can." In fact, he was so gracious he gave us his name and said, "If one of the ushers asks you why you are sitting there, you tell him that I gave you authority to do it." So we went down at halftime of the first game of a doubleheader. We sat behind the basket and, when the second half started, we noticed that there was a group of fellows in front of us who looked a little tall. We began to visit with them and discovered that they were the University of Louisville basketball club that had won the NCAA tournament the year before. Each of these boys was sporting a huge engraved ring set with a diamond. We struck up a conversation with two that were about our size—guards—and we talked to them. They said, "Man, that was a great year last year!" Then we asked them a question to which we already knew the answer: "How're you doing this year?" We knew it had been a bleak year. They said, "It's tough. We have won one-third of our ball games." And then one of them turned philosophical (even athletes can do that) and said, "When you're number one, everybody guns for you."

When you succeed, everybody wants to get you off the top of the mountain. Part of the perversity of human nature is that we don't like to see people above us. Elijah faced that perversity, and you will face it too.

Depression

"Elijah was afraid and ran for his life. When he came to Beersheba in Judah, he left his servant there, while he himself went a day's journey into the desert. He came to a broom tree, sat down under it and prayed that he might die. 'I have had enough, Lord,' he said. 'Take my life; I am no better than my ancestors.' Then he lay down under the tree and fell asleep" (1 Kings 19:3-5). One day he is on the mountain, and he is God's man. He is confident. He has been trusting God. He knows what God can do. The prophets of Baal are gathered there, and he challenges them. "Let's see whom we should worship." And his voice is strong—there is timbre in his voice, there is confidence in his soul. He mocks them while they are calling on their gods: "Oh, Baal, answer us." Elijah is walking around and saying, "Maybe your god is asleep. Maybe your god is busy, or maybe he is out visiting." Elijah, full of confidence, is mocking them. Four hundred and fifty of the enemy are there, and Elijah is alone on the mountain.

Then, when they have accomplished nothing—they have cut themselves, they have screamed, they have shouted, and the day is almost over—Elijah says, "Now it's my turn." He has the wood and the sacrificial animal, and he says, "Let's drench it. Let's make sure it's completely wet." He soaks the altar, digging a trench around it to gather the excess. Then he calls out to God, and God sends the fire, and it laps up the sacrifice and the wood and the stones and the dirt, and dries up the trenches.

The next day Elijah wants to die. The next day he says, "Lord, take me. It's over."

Why do we go through that? Are we sometimes Elijah revisited? What is there about the day after? I have known people who have finally received their doctor's degree, and the day after that great success they are depressed. I have known of couples who got married on a Friday night, and the next day was one of the worst days of their lives. Depression sometimes comes after that great and holy moment. You succeed triumphantly, you get your trophy, and the next day you are in the pits.

Why does that happen? Depression sometimes comes because we are exhausted. We have worked so hard, we have strained, we have stayed up late nights. We have invested our lives and energy, and finally we achieve our goal and then we are weary. Twice in 1 Kings 19, Elijah goes to sleep. He is simply fatigued. When you are tired, you are neither physically well nor spiritually strong. You get depressed easily.

There is such a contrast between being on the mountain and being in the valley. Remember when you went to that men's retreat and you had such a great experience? You prayed with men, and you were challenged, and you recommitted your life to Christ. You said, "My business is going to belong to the Lord, my devotional life is going to be strong, I'm going to tell my wife I love her; I am going to do all those things." It was a great and holy moment. And then you went down to the valley, and you were suddenly down in the dumps. Our young people do it at their retreats, women do it at their retreats. There is something about that high and holy moment and the contrast after it is over that is like the string on the violin which snaps after the concert. You have given your all, and afterwards there is only a *pop!*

What does God do to Elijah? He says, "Elijah, what are you doing here? Elijah, tell me, what is going on in your life? Would you like to talk about it?" Elijah opens up his heart and tells God how lonely he is and how defeated he feels. What does God do? God meets him not in the great storms but in that still, small voice. God meets him in the quietness. God does a work in his life. God meets him and reminds him of all of his resources. He says, "There are seven thousand others who have not bowed the knee. Rise up. There are people that pray for you, that want to live and share with you. I am available to you." After He allows him to ventilate and to be reminded of his resources both in God and in his people, He then says, "Go back to work." He gives Elijah some assignments to do. God says, "We are going to retread you, Elijah, and send you back to work." God knows how to deal with our depression—our depression that sometimes comes even after success.

The Proper Management of Success

I would like to suggest some ways in which we can handle our successes regardless of how small or how infrequent they may be. When they come, how do you handle them?

Celebrate the fact

Celebrate anything that is in the will of God. He wants you to enjoy it. Anything in His will is worth celebrating. The three parables in Luke 15 have a common thread: All three of them are about things that are lost. The first is the story of the lost sheep.

The shepherd has one hundred sheep; ninety-nine are safe, but one is lost. The shepherd goes out and looks and finally finds the one sheep and says, "Rejoice with me" (Luke 15:6). The second story is about a woman who has ten silver coins. She can only find nine; one is missing, so she cleans the house and looks under the rugs and under the furniture. She finally finds the silver coin and says to her neighbors and friends, "Rejoice with me" (Luke 15:9). The third story is about the prodigal son, the lost son. The father gives the son what he is entitled to, and the son goes to a far-off country. The father prays for him, and one day he is looking down the road and sees his wandering son coming back home. Ecstatic, the father puts a ring on his son's finger, a robe on his back, and says, "Kill the animal, let us celebrate! Let us have a feast!" Anything in the will of God is worth celebrating.

Two cautions, however: first make sure what you have accomplished is in the will of God. If you have achieved success by cheating, or by stepping on people en route to it, or by a shortcut that is unethical, you don't need celebration; you need confession. But if you have genuinely succeeded in the will of God, celebrate. Even if you succeed in evangelism, celebrate. In heaven they rejoice when evangelists are successful. Celebrate when people come to faith in Christ. If your straying child comes back to God, that is worth celebrating. If your business succeeds in the will of God, celebrate that. Anything in the will of God is worth celebrating.

The second thing is to celebrate in a small group. Don't celebrate with a large company. All three stories in Luke 15 concern people who are with their friends or neighbors and family. Most of the world can't handle your celebration. They are not particularly pleased that you have succeeded anyhow. But the people who know you, and who love you, and who have worked with you, and who pray for you—they are the ones with whom you celebrate. You rejoice, you weep, you share with the people who know you intimately and who love you and who care for you. With them you celebrate your successes because they have prayed with you through them. They have prevailed with you through all the failures en route to them. Rejoice with a small group, with those significant others in your life—not with everybody.

Praise the Lord

Regardless of what that success is, praise the Lord. Were you the valedictorian? Did you finally get on the dean's roll? Did you get a job? Did you get a promotion? Did you buy your own business? Did your stocks do well? Have you enjoyed a significant success? Did you praise the Lord for that? In 1 Thessalonians 5:18 we read, "Give thanks in all circumstances, for this is God's will for you in Christ Jesus." Your energy, your time, your opportunities are gifts of God. Turn from the trophy to the Giver of every good gift and say, "Thank you, Lord! I want to praise you for it!" There is nothing more fitting than a believer who is blessed and who turns from that blessing to the Giver of every good and perfect gift and praises Him for it.

I will never forget the day that Dr. Bob Smith was made an emeritus faculty member after a distinguished career as professor of philosophy at Bethel College in Saint Paul, Minnesota. The day he received all the accolades and recognition was embarrassing to him. Godly people are always embarrassed by praise. The rest of us handle it very well, but godly people get embarrassed. Dr. Bob was embarrassed, but after his admirers rehearsed all the good things he had done, after they talked about the students that loved him and to whom he had given coats and all kinds of gifts through the years, Dr. Bob stood before the mike and said something to this effect: "I want to lay all my trophies at the feet of my lovely Lord, who made possible anything significant in my life."

I found an uncommon tear working its way down my cheek that day, and I joined a number of others who were taken by his words and thought, "How better to live out our lives and receive what little acknowledgment may come and say, 'To God be the glory!' " When you are honored and when you succeed, take that trophy into the throne room and give it back to the King and say, "I praise you for it!" Some of you have succeeded marvelously, and all of us have succeeded at different points in our lives. In the midst of it do we look at ourselves and say, "Weren't we wise and bright, keen and gifted?" Or do we say, "Thanks to God. Isn't He good?" The latter is the proper management of success.

Store the trophy

After the celebration, don't repeat it. People get tired of hearing a rehearsal of your victories. Just before we moved from Whittier to San Diego, we began throwing out all kinds of things. Some we just threw out, and others we gave to neighbors. A good time to come around is when people move.

Some things go on the moving truck; some go in the garbage can; some go to the neighbors. As we were cleaning things out, I found a little trophy that I had won playing golf when I was seventeen years old. I looked at it and it was tarnished badly. I went over and put it in the garbage can. And then I thought: That is a parable about life. Something good comes along, you do fairly well, you gain acknowledgment . . . but it all tarnishes. You have to throw it out.

In our previous church I had ten very happy years as pastor. Some people in my present church have said, "I've heard enough about that former pastorate of yours, and if you tell us one more time about that place, we'll wish that you'd stayed there." One of my friends very wisely said, "It's as though someone's wife dies, and he remarries, and he keeps telling his second wife all about the first wife—the perfect woman, you see." The time comes for all of us to store our trophies. Paul said, "Forgetting what is behind and straining toward what is ahead" (Phil. 3:13). Although Paul had an enviable heritage and could pride himself on great achievements, he had the audacity to say, "Forgetting all of that, I move forward."

But mark this well: Store the trophy—don't destroy it. The day will come when you will return to your own prayer closet, take out the trophy with nobody around, and thank God. It may restore your spirits enough to go on for another day. Don't bring the trophy out and tell anybody else about it.

God will do good things in our lives and we rejoice. But we must move on. We can't live back there forever. Today is a new day with new opportunities. God has fresh things to do in all of us.

Accept the responsibility

"From everyone who has been given much, much will be demanded" (Luke 12:48). If God gives to you, He requires greater things from you. Those who suddenly achieve in the will of God are expected to do more. People expect more when you succeed, and our God who enables you to succeed expects you to be faithful with the new things that you have.

Some time ago, Gary Hallberg won a golf tournament at Torrey Pines in the Isuzu-Andy Williams San Diego Open. The first three days of the tournament Gary mentioned that when his two companions finished putting, everyone would walk to the next hole and he would have to putt with nobody watching. Nobody stayed to watch Gary Hallberg putt, because almost nobody knew Gary Hallberg. The fourth day he won that tournament. Now, all of a sudden, people are going to wait until he finishes his putt—because once you win your first PGA victory the expectation of the gallery goes up.

God does the same. If you achieve because of your administrative strengths, God expects you to use those strengths to His glory. Your gifts were given and your opportunities were provided so that they might be used. If you have the gift of teaching, you are to stir up that gift and use it to the blessing of all. To whom much is given, from him much is required. If you are blessed financially, God expects you to give far beyond what anybody else can give because you have more. What a privilege it is! God gives, but His expectations and our responsibility also accelerate. "It is required that those who have been given a trust must prove faithful" (1 Cor. 4:2). A steward is one to whom possessions have been committed. When God blesses, when God honors, God expects. With success comes responsibility and accountability.

Many of you enjoy success in one or more areas. What do you do with the successes that come to you? Do you handle them well? Do you become confident and arrogant, or are you humbled? Do you graciously accept success as a gracious gift of a loving God and give Him praise? Do you turn those trophies back to Him and say, "Lord, thank you. I want to honor you with them. How can I serve you?" May God grant you not only opportunities to succeed but the privileges in Christ to use them to give Him praise and to serve Him as you have never done before for Jesus' sake.

For Further Thought

1. Why do we expect so much from successful people?

2. Has success spoiled your relationship with God? with your church? with your family?

3. What do you dislike about successful people? Do you find yourself being guilty of the very same things?

4. Why not pause and thank God for the good things you enjoy out of His kindness.

Four

Fear of Death

First Corinthians 15:50-58 is a great resurrection narrative written by the Apostle Paul: "I declare to you, brothers, that flesh and blood cannot inherit the kingdom of God, nor does the perishable inherit the imperishable. Listen, I tell you a mystery: We will not all sleep, but we will all be changed—in a flash, in the twinkling of an eye, at the last trumpet. For the trumpet will sound, the dead will be raised imperishable, and we will be changed. For the perishable must clothe itself with the imperishable, and the mortal with immortality. When the perishable has been clothed with the imperishable, and the mortal with immortality, then the saying that is written will come true: 'Death has been swallowed up in victory. Where, O death, is your victory? Where, O death, is your sting?' The sting of death is sin, and the power of sin is the law. But thanks be to God! He gives us the victory through our Lord Jesus Christ. Therefore, my dear brothers, stand firm.

Let nothing move you. Always give yourselves fully to the work of the Lord, because you know that your labor in the Lord is not in vain."

All of us will die. The only possible way to avoid death is through the intervention of our Lord's second coming. Every statistic in our world is lower than 100 percent—with the exception of the statistic regarding death. The death rate is 100 percent. The writer of the book of Hebrews said, "Man is destined to die once" (9:27). But we are afraid of death. There is something about death that is terrifying, and we expose our fear in a variety of ways. We show it in our vocabulary. We used to talk about "graveyards," but now we call them "cemeteries." And many of them have names like Memory Gardens or Forest Lawn. It is almost as though we were trying to soften the harshness of death. We used to talk about "undertakers," then we called them "funeral directors"—but now a few of them prefer the title "mercy consultants." We used to talk about "death," but now we talk about "passing away." Somehow the vocabulary of death is an attempt on our part to soften our fear of it. We expose our fears about death by repressing the very idea of it. We don't like to talk about it. We avoid it if at all possible.

We avoid it also through humor, which is one way of handling fear. When you really fear something you try to make jokes about it. Have you noticed how often the undertaker—or the funeral director—becomes the brunt of jokes? Edgar N. Jackson says, "Perhaps he does not realize it, but one of his most useful functions is to give a focal point for the anxieties that can be released through the humor of which he is the target."[1]

It is a fearful thing to die. One of the reasons Jesus came was to "free those who all their lives were held in slavery by their fear of death" (Heb. 2:15). Jesus came to say, "Don't be afraid of it!" But how can we avoid fearing it? First Corinthians 15 gives us three helpful suggestions for coping with the fear of death.

Accept Our Humanity

"In Adam all die" (1 Cor. 15:22). We are in Adam. To be human is to be finite, and to be finite is to die. We will all die. We are not indestructible.

Paul Tillich was a philosopher/theologian who left us with two major problems: The first is his theology, and the second is that it is so incomprehensible that even when you think you understand it you often cannot believe it. Communication theorists talk about a "fog index." Tillich's writings require graduate training in philosophy, and even then you are not certain you understand him. But he has a couple of insights in the midst of all of his writings that are worth sharing. I want to share both of them, and that is all of Tillich you will need. The first is that he said, "Anxiety is the awareness of finitude." That is, the threat of non-being (death) produces anxiety; and the shadow of this touches all of our other anxieties and gives them power.[2] Tillich is saying that the major anxiety of "being" is "non-being." The major anxiety of life is death. The major anxiety that we face as we are moving through life is the fact that it shall end. That is the major anxiety that underlies and informs all the other anxieties of life. We need, therefore, to accept our finitude. Paul said it; the writer of the book of Hebrews said it. It is real—we are human, we die. How do you deal with that fact?

One way is to read the writings of those who have conquered death. Read Victor Frankl, the psychiatrist, who wrote *Man's Search for Being*. It is an excellent book. Dietrich Bonhoeffer and Helmut Thielieke, two German theologians, are also both worth reading. These three men had something in common. They all heard the whistling sound of bombs falling around them. They heard the crumbling of the earth beneath them. They saw the shattering of buildings and the brokenness of bodies, and placed many deceased loved ones in the ground. Those three men looked death in the face, head-on. Their writings speak with great confidence, because we can never face life until we accept death. They faced death, and it freed them up to live.

Go to funerals. When you are about five years of age you are ready to start to face the problem of death, that is what the experts tell us. By the age of six you certainly should have gone to a funeral. But we don't want that experience for our children. We protect them from it because we are afraid of it and of what it will do to them. The best way for them to deal with it, however, is to be there.

When my son Steve was six he went to a funeral—his very first. Mark, a four-year-old buddy of his, had died. We went over to the casket, I lifted Steve up, and he looked into the lifeless body of Mark. He looked at his face and said, "That lucky duck, he's with Jesus."

That's a strange way to talk about resurrection faith, isn't it? But when you begin to face death head-on, then you are freed up to live. Read the testimony of men like Joe Bayly who lost three sons—one at eighteen days after surgery, another at five years with leukemia; and the third at eighteen years after a sledding accident complicated by mild hemophilia.[3] Bayly says that the things that make us fearful are the things that are unknown. The minute you begin to face death, you are enabled then to live in Christ.

Death is a reality. Face it. Accept it. It is part of our faith.

Live with Vitality

I have always been surprised by 1 Corinthians 15:58. It almost seems like a postscript that you would add to a letter. The whole passage has been talking about Jesus' life, His death, His resurrection, the post-resurrection appearances. Then Paul says that mortality shall put on immortality, the perishable shall put on the imperishable, the trumpet shall sound, we shall be changed—a victorious, triumphant message. Finally he adds a PS: "Give yourself fully to the work of the Lord." You say, "Why is that there?"

I never understood that admonition until I took a close look at the context. I began to realize that Paul is making that statement in the light of resurrection faith, in the light of death. I became convinced that what he is saying is this: The best way to live and face death is to live and serve Christ with all your life.

Here is the second helpful sentence from Tillich: Some go about "avoiding the threat of non-being by avoiding being."[4] Or, in language that we understand, some defend themselves against the fear of death by not being fully alive. If you are only half alive, death is not much of a change. Some people walk through life fearful of death and therefore do not live fully. Once you begin to live life fully, then you can say as did Paul in Philippians 1:21: "For to me, to live is Christ and to die is gain." You cannot really face death until you are living fully. That is the way to face it triumphantly. If you are living with the fear of death you can't live dynamically, because then death is a magnificent change, and you can't handle that. So you live dying. Paul says rather that we should live in such a way that we die living, not that we live dying. Give your life fully to Jesus Christ, and then you will live it to the full. If death comes, welcome it. You have lived your life fully.

Stephen was a man who looked full into the face of death and was stoned triumphantly. He had given life all that he had. He had burned out his life for the Saviour. When death came, Stephen did not fear it because he was living life to the full—and therefore he could face death.

The same was true of the Twelve. The disciples tended to live in first gear. They went up and down, and there was an undulation about their faith that was both disturbing and exhausting. You say, "Did they ever get it all together?" Not until Christ was resurrected—and then all of a sudden the remaining eleven of them went into overdrive. They lived their lives as firebrands from that day forward. Ten of the eleven died as martyrs—unafraid, unashamed.

When you live life to the full, death is not an enemy. That is why Paul puts it at the very end of his resurrection passage. Give your life to God.

Serve Him fully. Serve Him with great vitality and then you need not fear death. Die living; don't live dying.

Claim the Victory

"Thanks be to God! He gives us the victory through our Lord Jesus Christ" (1 Cor. 15:57). Jesus Christ lived, died, rose again, and conquered as the victorious Christ. His victory is our victory. His victory destroyed the three most unnerving fears that we have about death.

Being alone

People say, "I don't want to die. I can't handle that—the aloneness of it." A pastor writes of his own son's death. The little fellow had a premature death because of cancer. His dad was in the hospital room with him. The boy looked up into his dad's face and said, "Dad, am I going to die?" Dad choked back his tears and looked into his son's face and said, "Yes, son, that is what the doctors say. Are you afraid?" The little guy then said, "No, I am not afraid, but I wish someone else could die with me." That small boy captured in a few words what is so fearful for people: We die alone.

But not quite! "Even though I walk through the valley of the shadow of death, I will fear no evil, for you are with me" (Ps. 23:4). Jesus goes before us. He knows us by name, and He goes before us. As the song puts it, "I won't have to cross Jordan alone." The child of God goes with the Saviour.

Fear of the unknown

We don't know much about death and what happens right after death. A few little windows in

Scripture give us a peek here and a peek there, but we don't know all the details. There is a lot that is unknown. Have you ever wished that Lazarus had written a New Testament book? After the Lord brought him back from death, wouldn't it have been wonderful if the Spirit of God had inspired the Gospel According to Lazarus? We would have had that tantalizing peek into the other side. But the Holy Spirit chose not to give us that glimpse, so death remains something of an unknown quantity.

We do have a few "knowns," however. We know that we shall be with Him—immediately. People who were with us just a few days ago are now gone, but are there with Him. Jesus told the thief, "TODAY you will be with me in paradise" (Luke 23:43). To be absent from the body is to be present with the Lord. That is certain and immediate. That is one of the "knowns." A second is that we will fellowship with other believers (Luke 13:28-29). Dean Stanley had his wife's tombstone engraved with the words, "Till death us unite." Death brings us all back together again. The third thing we know is that when we are there, all that is a problem here will be gone. Never again will you have April 15, tears, pain, suffering, loneliness. Read Revelation 21. Freedom from hardship is the triumph of His resurrection.

The fear of judgment

Do you know why we have such fear? Because we know our own hearts. If you know you and I know me, we ought to fear judgment. To have all of that exposed—all the things we have thought, all the things we have said, all the things we have left undone—and all the things we have done! All of that—to be judged for it! No wonder people are afraid of death. But Paul reminds us that "being justified by faith we have peace with God." He also says, "There is now no condemnation for those who are in Christ Jesus" (Rom. 8:1). There is no judgment for sin for the believer. His sins have already been covered. That is what Calvary is all about. All the judgment was absorbed by Jesus' body. He accepted our judgment. That is what vicarious atonement is all about. The only judgment you and I will face as believers is for works and for rewards—works that will give us rewards. The judgment for sin for the believer has already occurred. "There is now no condemnation for those who are in Christ Jesus."

If you fear death it may be that you need to look again into the Word of God and claim the fact that death is inevitable; but when you live life to the full and claim His victory, you can face it unashamed and unafraid.

Or it may be that you ought to be afraid, because if you have never trusted Christ as Saviour, it is a fearful thing to fall into the hands of an angry, righteous God.

For Further Thought

1. Are you afraid to die? What is there about death that is fearful for you?

2. Are you celebrating life to the full? If not, why not? (Remember John 10:10.)

3. If you are a Christian, thank God for His victory over death. If you have never trusted Christ as personal Saviour, would you be willing to do that right now? It's the best decision you will ever make.

Notes

1. Edgar N. Jackson, *For the Living* (Des Moines: Channel Press, 1963), p. 81.
2. Quoted by Howard Clinebell, *Basic Types of Pastoral Counseling* (Nashville: Abingdon Press, 1966), pp. 248-249.
3. Joseph Bayly, *The Last Thing We Talk About* (Elgin, IL: David C. Cook Publishing Co., 1973).
4. Clinebell, *Basic Types*, p. 249.

Five

Marriage

Marriage is God's invention. It was God's idea in the first place. He decided that a man and a woman should come together in a lifelong relationship that continues to grow and be fulfilled and become mutually enriching.

How is your marriage? How is it going? You don't have to be a sociologist to realize that marriage in America has fallen on hard times. We have all kinds of options, don't we? About two million American people are living with each other—without going through the ceremony of marriage. They are just living together. We have homosexual marriages. We have group marriages. More than two million people will get divorced in 1983—three times the percentage of fifty years ago. How is your marriage?

Amazingly enough, the sociologists are encouraged. I have just been reviewing a number of books written about marriage in the last three to five years. Leslie and Leslie remind us that in 1920, 58 percent of adult Americans got married. In the 1970s, the figure had risen to 75 percent. Do you know that in 1983, the statistic is that 95 percent of all adult Americans will be married at least once in their lifetime? The marriages may not be long, and they may not be good. But 95 percent of all adults will be married at some point.[1] The sociologists are agreed that marriage is here to stay.

You say, "Isn't that good! People are catching on to God's idea." Well, not completely. If people are marrying more than ever, they are also divorcing each other much more frequently.[2]

Problems for the Married

Marriage is here to stay but, strangely enough, marriages are deteriorating. The institution is here, but the relationships are eroding. Why? Let me suggest four areas of concern that all of us must face squarely.

People change

I don't know how long it is since you and your mate exchanged vows. That was a good day, I trust. But a lot has happened since then. If it was ten or twenty-five years ago, you know that the woman you married or the man you married is a different person today. If you are alive and well, you will change.

Unfortunately, people don't always change together and at the same pace. Sometimes because of one's vocation a person gets farther and farther away from his or her mate. Or perhaps a woman decides to further her education, and her husband chooses not to. She begins to live in a different world of thoughts and ideas, she gains new horizons that she never had before, and soon communication between man and wife breaks down. Or it could be that one is making a lot of money and one isn't. They begin to move in different circles, and soon they have separate bank accounts, which only compounds the problem.

People change. And if they don't change together, they are headed for trouble and possible divorce. "Irreconcilable differences" is a phrase used when some marriages fail. People change. Sometimes the very characteristic that seemed so attractive before marriage becomes irritating later on. "She married him because he was 'dominant and strong'; she divorced him because he was so 'domineering.' He married her because she was 'petite and feminine'; he divorced her because she was 'weak and helpless.' She married him because 'he could provide a living'; she divorced him because 'all he did was work, work, work.' He married her because she was 'fun-loving and a free spirit'; he divorced her because she was 'lazy and irresponsible.' "[3]

People change, perceptions change, attitudes change—and unless you change together, your marriage may be headed for disaster.

Media images

Turn on the television and you will discover that it is not broadcasting good, wholesome man/woman/husband/wife relationships that are pure, loving and growing. Instead you get musical mates, and infidelity becomes the expected. It doesn't matter whether it is a daytime soap, or a nighttime soap like *Dynasty* or *Dallas,* or a number of other programs that all sound alike. They are all saying similar things: Embrace an alternate life-style.

The Bible uses a synonym for "alternate life-style." It is called "sin." You see a man and a woman talking together and he says, "But I'm married." And she says, "Aren't we all?" And away they go with their little affair. If you see that sort of thing long enough, you get over the shock of it. As you continue to watch, it begins to tattoo your subconscious. Soon you think you are unusual because you have been with the same mate for thirty years. Have you lost your excitement? Everybody else tells you, "That's the way it is." Media images can do a disservice to your attitudes and principles. Marshall McLuhan says we become what we behold. If he is right, we are all in big trouble.

Financial crunch

If you bought a home eighteen years ago, you may have a house payment of about $120 per month. If you sell your home to a newly married couple—if the couple can qualify for a mortgage with both of them working—it will probably cost them $1,000 a month for the same house. You bought it for $18,000; it now sells for $132,000, and interest rates have exploded.

How fortunate you are if you purchased a home many years ago! We used to tell couples, "Never spend over 25 percent of your income for your house, your utilities, your insurance, and your taxes." If we tell that to young people today, they think we are talking nonsense. The average couple that I have married in the last three years spends about $800 a month on house payments. And that is for a "starter" home, a four-room house. So both of them have to work full time, and the pressures on them are heavy indeed.

Sixty percent of one's income for housing is a very common figure these days. And you don't have to be young to face it. A lot of people confront that kind of financial crunch, and it hits them in one way or another. Such a wedge can drive a marriage apart. Many people cannot handle that kind of financial pressure.

Secular humanism

I am not quite so pessimistic on this fourth concern as some evangelical writers are, because you could do worse than have a secular humanist as your neighbor. He will probably be honest, and he will probably not rob you of your home. He probably will keep his property in good shape, and he probably won't cheat you. But I find it incredible that anybody can live without God in his world view. To think that some people live their whole lives without God to inform them, to empower them, to enable them!

On a recent Sunday night after church I turned on the television set and heard a lecture from a man I had heard and read about but had never seen before. His name is Leo Buscaglia. He is a teacher at the University of Southern California. Again and again he has been chosen "Teacher of the Year" at that institution. He has written a book that is high on the best-seller nonfiction list: *Living, Loving and Learning.*[5] For forty-five minutes he enthralled me. A tantalizing communicator, he has a great sense of humor. He was speaking in a lecture hall at Harvard and had his audience eating out of his hand. He was talking about love talk. So I went out and bought his book. But as I read through it I was stunned to discover that in 264 pages of writing about love, not once did he refer to the love of God or the love of Christ. That is secular humanism. That is looking at love without the One who is the power for love, without the One in whom love finds its birth. You can only reflect God's love. You cannot initiate it or create it. God's love—Christ's love—how terrible to live without that! Marriage cannot exist in health and vitality on secular humanism. I don't know how a non-Christian couple makes it. Marriages between unbelievers can hold together only through common grace.

Help for the Married

People changes represent the social dimension, *media images* the physical, *financial problems* the economic, and *secular humanism* the spiritual. Those are the four dimensions on which every marriage is built. And those are the four areas in which deterioration comes most quickly.

Hebrews 13 either directly or indirectly refers to those four areas. The writer is concluding his great book with a cluster of exhortations. Let's look at them in the light of marriage and examine them as principles applicable to marriage.

Be friends

The way to respond to the social dimension is to be friends. "Keep on loving each other as brothers" (Heb. 13:1). The implication is this: "You have been friends; continue to be friends and make it your great desire." The word in the Greek is *phila-*

delphia, "brotherly love," from which the city on the East Coast is named. It is the love of friendship; it is the love of sharing and caring. It is not erotic love or romantic love or agape love, but it is the love of friends who share their lives together. The writer says, "Keep on being friends, just as you always have been."

What about marriage? What about your friend's marriage? Do you remember how it was when you were dating? You were on the phone by the hour. You would take long walks. You would talk to each other. Time passed quickly when you were together. He or she was your dearest, closest friend in all the world. And now you are married, and something has happened.

A lady in a restaurant noticed a couple and turned to her friend and said, "They are not married." Her friend said, "How do you know that?" She said, "He is listening to her." At the breakfast table too many wives know the back side of a newspaper and not the front side of a face. She and her husband simply grunt at each other.

Nancy and I attended Wheaton College three decades ago. Our president, Dr. V. Raymond Edman, was an extraordinary man with a gifted pen and a quaint way of expressing himself. Two of his favorite expressions are unforgettable. He referred to his pet as "brown dog," and to his mate as "friend wife." That latter phrase stuck in my mind, and for almost twenty-five years I have used it to refer to the special lady who bears my name and shares my mortgage. I am grateful today that she is my closest friend in all the world. There is nobody nearly as close to me as "friend wife."

That shouldn't be unusual for any man. That

ought to be the normal thing. When you get home at night, you find yourself saying, "Hey, hon, listen to this . . . " And you tell her about your day. And then it is her turn and she tells you about her day, and if you have had a problem you share it, and she says, "Oh, I understand!" You are friends and you talk to each other. There is no hidden agenda.

Do you know how to build that kind of relationship? Through conflict! Conflict management is a stepping stone to enriching a friendship. If all you do is breathe, you will still have conflicts. When I see a couple that has never had a conflict, one of them has given up. That is not unity; that is conformity. Don't be afraid to think. Share your thoughts with each other. Deal with conflict and face it together in Christ. Move ahead in your friendship.

Someone has said, "We need to learn how to 'fight' as Christian couples." Here are the rules: (1) If you are a friend and you love her, deal with issues and avoid name-calling. (2) Take responsibility. When you go into a difficult situation, don't say, "You make me mad." Instead say, "Would you help me deal with a problem I have?" Assume responsibility. Work your way through the problem in honesty and candor. Deal with all the issues; get them out in the open so that they ventilate and breathe. And don't forget, the best way for a married couple to conclude a fight is in a clinch.

The resolution of a relationship that has gone through tough times can be one of the most beautiful things in a marriage. I have enjoyed many such resolutions. If conflicts come into your life and in the will of God you can deal with them, you can emerge enriched in your friendship with your spouse so that your best friend in the world will be your mate.

Be lovers

Principle number two is the physical dimension in a marriage. "Marriage should be honored by all, and the marriage bed kept pure, for God will judge the adulterer and all the sexually immoral" (Heb. 13:4). Guard yourself against all adulterous possibilities. The best defense is a strong offense. I have seen marriages deteriorate morally because of illicit affairs, and that often happens because there is some sort of vacuum in the relationship, and a person chooses the wrong way to fill it. Be lovers.

There are a number of Greek words that describe love. One is found in Hebrews 13:1: "Keep on loving each other"—*phileo*, related to *philadelphia*, brotherly love, the love of friends. The second is *agape*—the love found in Ephesians 5:25: "Husbands, love your wives, just as Christ loved the church." *Agape* love is unconditional and giving. It is not the love of emotion but the love of the will. You must choose to love, to do the loving thing. *Agape* love says, "Christ loved the church and gave Himself for her." *Agape* love says, "What is the loving thing?" and then goes out of its way and does it simply because it loves. Every marriage needs that. The third kind of love is *eros*—romantic love. Such love is legitimate between a man and a woman who are married. It is what Dr. Ed Wheat describes as "that which transforms a black and white existence into glorious, living technicolor."[6] Satan's perversion is technique-ridden, and there are all kinds of books available that are simply the devil's perversion. They are books about human plumbing, not about love. When God says, "The two shall become one flesh," He is referring to the love between a man and a woman who are married and who enjoy what He has provided.

Build a relationship in all three of these areas. Be lovers. Keep your marriage healthy and vital and growing.

Be content

This principle of being content relates to the financial dimension. "Keep your lives free from the love of money and be content with what you have, because God has said, 'Never will I leave you, never will I forsake you' " (Heb. 13:5).

Incredible things happen to marriages when financial pressures come. I was once awakened at 3:00 in the morning to go and counsel a couple. They couldn't even wait until 7:00. They had to deal with their problem immediately. They had been up with it all night, and they wanted me to help them out. And so we sat and talked about their financial problems. My usual advice is this: "For openers cut up your credit cards." People today are living in a fantasy world. They see something, they want it, they buy it, and then the bill comes. Keep credit cards only for emergencies, and keep your credit rating up. But live realistically.

"Be content with what you have." God has promised never to leave you or forsake you. Matthew 6:33 is right to the point: "Seek first his kingdom and his righteousness, and all these things will be given to you as well." God says, "Get your priorities straight; I will take care of your needs.

You can trust me for that." Don't have that insatiable desire to have and to have and to have. It will destroy you. Learn contentment. Find rest in God. He will provide for your needs. Be a good worker. God has His hand on you, and He can be trusted. Find contentment in Him.

Be dependent

"So we say with confidence, 'The Lord is my helper; I will not be afraid. What can man do to me?' " (Heb. 13:6). "The Lord is my helper." I would like to suggest that being dependent upon God is the spiritual dimension to marriage.

Hebrews 13:6 is a quotation from Psalm 118. The historical point of reference for Psalm 118 is either the finishing of the second Temple under Zerubbabel or the completion of the city wall under Nehemiah. Regardless of which you choose, both are post-exilic, both talk about great conflicts and problems faced by the people of God, and both talk about the resolution of the project in the will of God. When the returning Jews were building the Temple, the Samaritans gave them problems. When they were building the wall under Nehemiah, everybody was giving them problems. God is saying, "In the midst of your trials and your projects, I will enable and I will strengthen." Am I spiritualizing the text too much to suggest that when you build a marriage, the same provision is available? God is my helper, God is my strength, God will put us together, God will be the "cement"; and through brokenness and tears we must turn to Him and say, "God, we have made a mess of this thing! Help us! Lord, strengthen our marriage!"

Our marriages need God as the "cement" that

binds them. Dwight Small has written, "A good marriage links the very power of God to the marriage union."[7] God invented it; He can empower it. He can enable you. The same Christ who can redeem a soul can redeem a marriage. God can turn everything around and make it new. Wherever you are in your marriage, He is able. "No temptation has seized you except what is common to man. And God is faithful" (1 Cor. 10:13). That applies to your marriage just as it does to any other area of life.

Your marriage can be made whole again. It may hurt, and it may take counsel, and it may take the love and support of friends, and it may require a radical change in your life. But God is committed to your marriage, to your life together. Would you trust Him for that? His idea is that two people should live their lives together in a mutually enriching and fulfilling relationship that brings joy to your hearts and pleasure to the heart of our God.

For Further Thought

1. What is the biggest problem you face in your marriage? Are you working at solving it? If not, why not?

2. Is your mate your friend? He or she could be. Try it, will you?

3. Have you learned contentment? What does it take to be satisfied with what you have?

4. Have you reaffirmed your vows with your mate recently? Why not do it soon?

Notes

1. Gerald R. Leslie and Elisabeth Leslie, *Marriage in a Changing World* (New York: John Wiley & Sons, 1980), p. 5.
2. Ibid.
3. J. Mark Platt, "The Family Tree," published by Berryessa Evangelical Free Church, n.d.
4. Marshall McLuhan, *The Medium Is the Massage* (New York: Bantam Books, 1967).
5. Leo Buscaglia, *Living, Loving, and Learning* (Thorofare, NJ: Charles B. Slack, Inc., 1982).
6. Ed Wheat, *Love Life* (Grand Rapids: Zondervan Publishing House, 1980), p. 60.
7. Dwight Small, *Your Marriage Is God's Affair* (Old Tappan, New Jersey: Fleming Revell, 1979), p. 9.

Six

Divorce

"To the married I give this command (not I, but the Lord): A wife must not separate from her husband. But if she does, she must remain unmarried or else be reconciled to her husband. And a husband must not divorce his wife. To the rest I say this (I, not the Lord): If any brother has a wife who is not a believer and she is willing to live with him, he must not divorce her. And if a woman has a husband who is not a believer and he is willing to live with her, she must not divorce him. For the unbelieving husband has been sanctified through his wife, and the unbelieving wife has been sanctified through her believing husband. Otherwise your children would be unclean; but as it is, they are holy. But if the unbeliever leaves, let him do so. A believing man or woman is not bound in such circumstances; God has called us to live in peace" (1 Cor. 7:10-15).

We live in an age of disposable relationships. Marriages nowadays don't last. Occasionally a couple will even rewrite their vows so that they say "till love us do part" instead of "till death us do part." They build their marriage on the tenuousness and fragility of emotion and feeling. Some have suggested that we are moving very quickly to the day when we will add divorce to death and taxes as inevitable parts of American life. In the 1800s there was only one divorce for every twenty-one marriages. By 1900 it had gone to one for twelve; by World War I, one for ten; by 1940, one for five; by 1950, one for four; today, the ratio is one for three.[1]

Why do people disavow the vow that God has called them to make? "What God has joined together, let man not separate" (Matt. 19:6). And yet they separate, and separate, and separate.

Nobody really wants divorce. It is painful. It is socially awkward. It is lonely. And yet the drumbeat goes on, and divorces accelerate.

According to a recent study of six hundred divorcing couples, the first complaint of the group was mental cruelty. Then came neglect of home and children, then financial problems, then physical abuse, then drinking, then infidelity, then verbal abuse, then lack of love, then sexual incompatibility, and—last of all—in-law trouble.[2]

Stages in the Divorce Process

Elizabeth Kübler-Ross, who has written very helpfully about the nature of grief, says that people go through stages in grief.[3] The same thing happens with respect to divorce. People go through stages. Reva S. Wiseman says that there are five stages that divorced people go through. They are as follows:[4]

The first stage is denial. That takes place when an emotional divorce occurs but a denial of it allows the marriage to continue. There is no emotional support and there is no love reinforcement. But there is a public denial of it, as if everything was fine. Perhaps by now, however, the man and woman are living in separate bedrooms. There is no physical intimacy between them anymore.

The second stage is loss and depression. The reality of the separation strikes the couple, and they try to make peace with that fact. One woman wrote as follows: "When my husband told me he was leaving, numbness set in and I felt wrapped in cotton. I felt as though I were wearing a neon sign which flashed the message, 'I am a Failure.' "[5]

The third stage is anger and ambivalence. Depression turns to hostility and bitterness, the bitterness that arises over division of property, alimony, child support, and other matters. The couple becomes very bitter, and the battleground becomes a place of accusation and assassination of character. But yet ambivalence arises, and you say, "Am I at fault? Is there something I can still do? Where can I turn?"

The fourth stage is reorientation. The big question now is, "Who am I? Am I single or am I married?" You go to singles groups, and they are talking about things that don't quite interest you yet. In your mind you are still married. You go to meetings of married people, and there are couples there, and you are alone. You are in the demilitarized zone between the two areas. You are not sure where you fit. The time of reorientation is a lonely time. Before, you turned over in bed and there was a lovely head next to yours. You would put your arm around her and squeeze her. But now you turn over and the pillow is empty. You used to go down to breakfast and look into his face, but now no one is there. You used to rush home from work and say, "I had the craziest experience"—now you find that you are talking to yourself. The ceiling lowers and the walls enclose you, and you feel imprisoned in the loneliness of being single. For the first time you may be looking for a full-time job. You married young and he went to work and you stayed home. Then the children arrived, and you never entered the job market. But now here you are, forty-four years old and looking for your first full-time job. You feel a bit lonely out there, selling yourself to employment agencies and personnel directors and saying, "I need a job." They say, "What are your skills?" You say, "I need a job. I don't know what my skills are. I cook, I keep a nice house—I'm not too sure what my skills are." It can be a very traumatic time.

The final stage is acceptance. You acknowledge your new identity and, generally, find forgiveness and restoration as a Christian and feel accepted by the Lord. The anger has subsided, the new identity begins to be comfortable, you have won new friends and a new life has begun.

Biblical Standards for Remarriage
Let's look now at the biblical standards for remarriage. Are there any? Chuck Swindoll, in his book *Strike the Original Match*, teaches that there are three biblical circumstances where divorce and then remarriage are permitted.[6] In a variety of ways he says that divorce is never commanded, required, or suggested, but it is permitted biblically.

The first circumstance—divorce before conversion: "If anyone is in Christ, he is a new creation; the old has gone, the new has come!" (2 Cor. 5:17). If Calvary covers everything, Calvary covers divorce before you became a Christian. All that happened before your conversion experience is under the blood of the Lamb. You are now a new creature and start life again in the will of God.

The second circumstance—adultery: The Pharisees came to Jesus to test Him, and they asked, "Is it lawful for a man to divorce his wife for any and every reason?" Jesus answered, "I tell you that anyone who divorces his wife, except for marital unfaithfulness, and marries another woman commits adultery" (Matt. 19:3,9).

The Pharisees' question, of course, relates to divorce, and so does Jesus' answer. Jesus says, "When two people come together, they become one flesh." That is what it says in the Genesis creation account. Jesus reiterates it, and Paul talks about it again in Ephesians 5. When the one flesh has been broken, and the mate goes out and becomes one flesh with someone else, then the innocent party who has been sinned against is free to remarry. We do well to remember, however, that it is not commanded; it is only permitted.

I have known situations, perhaps as you have, in which a couple had shared their life together, and then one got careless and became unfaithful. The other person kept pure during the entire time. The Christian thing to do is to offer grace and forgiveness. I am reminded of the story of Hosea, who married a woman named Gomer. She went out and began to sleep with the men of the town, and she had children by two of them. But Hosea lovingly brought her back into his home and restored her—just as God restores us. That kind of forgiveness can take place. That certainly needs to be offered. It is a big step of humility and grace for one who has been sinned against to do that, but it ought to be attempted. But if reconciliation is impossible, freedom to remarry is a permitted option.

The third circumstance—marriage to an unbeliever: 1 Corinthians 7 tells about a believer married to an unbeliever. If the man has an unbelieving wife, and if she wants to stay, he should keep her. If the woman has an unbelieving husband, and he chooses to stay, she should keep him. His or her presence as the believing mate sanctifies that marriage. God grants blessing in that home because of the presence of that believer. "But if the unbeliever leaves" (1 Cor. 7:15)—that is, if he or she deserts, wants out of the marriage, wants nothing to do with it—let him or her go. A believing man or woman is not "bound" in such circumstances.

In verse 39, the same word "bound" is found. A woman is bound to her husband as long as he lives, but if her husband dies she is free to marry anyone she wishes—but he must belong to the Lord. The Greek word for "bound" is related to the Greek word for slave—*doulos*—and means that as long as they are married they are bound together. When death comes they are free to marry again.

If the unbelieving departs, you are no longer bound—you are released—because "God has called us to live in peace" (1 Cor. 7:15). What does that mean? Simply this: If the unbeliever leaves, the believer is to release him if he chooses not to stay. The believer is to allow him to be released, to be divorced, and not to hang on for dear life as if such divorce is the non-Christian thing to do. The divorce is the Christian thing in this case—but only in this setting where it is commanded.

A tragedy that often occurs is that the unbeliever goes his or her separate way and the believer thinks that somehow there is nothing right about divorce under any circumstances. People will hang on for years, and perhaps for a lifetime. But the Word of God says, "God has called you to peace—settle that thing." You are not the guilty one; you are releasing the guilty party, and you have biblical permission to do so. Don't hang on.

There is a fourth circumstance to add to Swindoll's three. Jay E. Adams has written a helpful book entitled *Marriage, Divorce and Remarriage in the Bible.*[7] He deals with all of the steps we have mentioned, and he is extremely concerned that we are often not very biblical in these matters. He feels that everything must be checked out biblically rather than emotionally. What happens when people get a divorce without biblical reasons? Can they remarry? Adams says, "There are many wrong attitudes in the conservative churches about divorce and divorcees. From the way that some treat divorced persons, you would think they had committed the unpardonable sin. Let us make it clear, then, that those who wrongly (sinfully) obtain a divorce must not be excused for what they have done; it *is* sin. But precisely because it is sin, it is forgivable. The sin of divorcing one's mate on Biblical grounds is bad not only because of the misery it occasions, but especially because it is an offense against a holy God. But it is not so indelibly imprinted in the life of a sinner that it cannot be washed away by Christ's blood."[8] He continues, "Since divorce is not the unpardonable sin, it can be forgiven. That, of course, does not heal all the heartbreaks of children and in-laws, not to speak of the parties involved in the divorce. I don't mean to say that it does. Divorce, even when proper, always is occasioned by someone's sin. At its best, then, divorce always brings misery and hurt. That is why God hates it. But even one who sinfully obtains a divorce can be forgiven, cleansed and restored to Christ's church just like those repentant drunkards and homosexuals who are mentioned in 1 Corinthians 6:9-11. They, too, can be washed and sanctified by the same Spirit. We must not call unclean those whom God has cleansed! When Jesus spoke about the unpardonable sin, He carefully assured us about the forgivability of other sins—all other sins—when He declared: 'All sorts of sins and blasphemies will be forgiven' . . . (Matt. 12:31). All other sins can be forgiven. And since obtaining a divorce for sinful reasons falls into that category, we must conclude that it too is a forgivable sin."[9]

Here is a final quote from Adams: "Now someone will say that makes forgiveness too easy and will encourage divorce. I do not honor that argument any more than Paul did in Romans. Divorce, wrongly obtained is sin—a heinous offense against God and man. I am not encouraging divorce any more than God encouraged robbery, adultery, homosexuality, lying and murder by declaring that such sins are totally forgiven in Christ and put into the past (1 Corinthians 6:11). Repentance, when genuine, is like David's repentance (Psalms 51, 38 etc.); it is not treated lightly as a gimmick. A repentant sinner recognizes the serious nature of his offense and is not only grateful but produces fruit (change) appropriate to repentance. In any discussion of divorce and remarriage, we must be careful to preserve the integrity of two Biblical truths: 1. Sin is heinous. 2. Grace is greater than the most heinous sin (Rom. 5:20). So we have seen that remarriage after divorce is allowed in the Bible and that the guilty party after forgiveness is free to remarry."[10]

This is a complex and difficult circumstance indeed. I trust that if you are in that situation you will prayerfully consider the nature of forgiveness and the nature of repentance and that you will seek not only to forgive yourself but to find God's forgiveness. Then go to your mate and seek his or her forgiveness, and then forgive him or her. Calvary can deal with the toughest problem.

Steps Back to Health

What about those who are divorced? What are the steps back to spiritual and emotional health? Let me suggest some biblical principles.

Walk through it

No one can walk through a divorce situation for you. People can pray with you, they can share with you, they can listen to you, they can encourage you—but only you can walk through it. At times you will feel desperately alone, but keep walking. God has not changed. "Jesus Christ is the same" (Heb. 13:8) as when you were married. He is the same today, and He will be the same forever. You can claim His unchangeableness even as you continue to change. It generally takes two years to work through a divorce—about the same length of time it takes to work through the death of a spouse. It is hard, but keep walking.

Accept the facts

Don't deny the fact of your divorce—you are now single. Some denial practices are very destructive. One of them is *dating questionable people.* I knew a husband and wife who were cautious and careful and caring and obedient. They got a divorce, and then one of them suddenly dated strange people—people in bars and other questionable places of one sort or another. The second denial practice is *reckless spending*—as if by spending enough you forget about being single. That doesn't solve anything. A third is *excessive socializing.* Sometimes divorced people begin to drink or turn to drugs and sleeping pills. A fourth is *over-absorption at work.* Once married to someone they now become married to the job. Such a denial practice does not produce spiritual or mental health.

Remember that you may no longer be his, but you are still His (Eph. 4). Your new situation does not change your old relationship to Him. As a child of God you still belong to Him. You may not belong to the one who used to bear your name, but you still belong to Him who is your Saviour. Accept that fact.

Live in the present

"If we confess our sins, he is faithful and just and will forgive us our sins and purify us from all unrighteousness" (1 John 1:9). Don't live with sin unforgiven. Deal with it; claim Calvary; claim the cross; claim what Jesus Christ did for you. Get it cared for. Then, forgetting the things that are behind, move forward (see Phil. 3:13-14).

We all fail. Some of us fail in one area, some in another. Some will fail in their marriage. Some will fail in their attitude. Church has sometimes been easier on those who gossip than on those who are divorced, but the Bible treats gossip as it does divorce. We all fail, but no failure needs to be final. By God's grace we can be forgiven, we can be cleansed, we can be made new.

Associate with healthy people

When you have physical problems, you turn to an M.D. When you have emotional problems, you may turn to a psychologist, a therapist—God's instruments of healing, tools used by our God to help you to understand yourself and help restore you to emotional health again. Turn to those who can encourage your health. Turn to people who are growing. It is counterproductive to associate only with people who are going through the same problem you are but who are having no success with it. You share war stories together, and sometimes that can be painful: "If you think your husband mistreated you, let me tell you my story!" They get worse and worse, so you begin to create stories that sound bad enough to be accepted.

Being with people who are in the midst of pain may not encourage your health. Associate with people who are struggling but who are growing. Growing is so necessary. You need the healing encouragement of people who are being healed and who are not simply exchanging pathologies.

Take time to grow

Get into the Word of God and begin to claim the resources of God in Christ Jesus. If you have lived without Him, you need Him and His Word and the help you gain from it. Take time to be holy. Take time to pray. Take time to attend retreats and seminars where God's Word and God's people can continue to minister to you.

Get busy again for God

"As it is, there are many parts, but one body. The eye cannot say to the hand, 'I don't need you!' And the head cannot say to the feet, 'I don't need you!' " (1 Cor. 12:20-21). Paul says that all the parts of the Body are necessary so that the married cannot say to the divorced, "I don't need you." If the Spirit of God has given gifts to the entire Body of Christ, then the entire Body of Christ should use its gifts for the health of the Church. When there are divorced people who are not using their gifts, the Body of Christ suffers. Ask for forgiveness! Be restored! Use your gifts again!

I know a couple who are divorced, and for years they felt that they could never serve God again because of it. When we began to study the Word of God together, they discovered that the people of God were putting pressure on them—not the Word of God. The text in 1 Timothy 3 that speaks of the "husband of one wife" is not a divorce text. It is talking about purity, about a one-woman kind of man who lives with purity. It does not say anything about divorce. Once cleansed, once forgiven, begin to serve God again. The Body of Christ needs you.

If you are single you are saying, "I don't need to

learn about divorce and remarriage." But let me say this to you. If you are single, carefully consider what it means to marry a Christian, one to whom you can commit your entire life and with whom you can live together in the will of God. Don't be thoughtless or quick. Be wise, be sensitive, accept Christian advice. Check and pray and consider. And if you marry, look into the face of the one to whom you are going to commit yourself for life and say, "We are going to share our life together in Christ."

If you are married, I would, first of all, ask that you *show grace as you deal with the divorced.* We can be so thoughtless about the things we say and the attitudes we share with those who have gone through divorce. I have heard preachers who lash out against it, and then their own children get divorced and suddenly they become gracious again. I have seen people change under the impact of the pain in their own homes. I remember a man—a strong Christian leader—whose wife divorced him. In great suffering and agony he told me, "Pastor, help people never to throw stones; someday they will live in glass houses." So, to you who are married and whose marriage is good, be grateful. This is not the time to lash out.

Second, *keep working at your own marriage.* Thank God for good marriages, but be gracious to those who have gone through the problems.

If you are divorced, I want you to know that although sin occasions it, and there is great heartache and grief in connection with it, Calvary can deal with that. I love you, and much more importantly, God loves you. You can be restored, and God can use you again. That is what Calvary is all about. Would you claim that?

For Further Thought

1. What are the stages that divorced people tend to move through?

2. How do you relate to those who are divorced? Are you compassionate? judgmental? aloof?

3. What should your attitude be regarding remarriage of the divorced? What does the Bible say?

4. If you are divorced, have you moved through it? God's people need you and God loves you . . . will you claim those facts?

Notes

1. James M. Henslin, ed., *Marriage and Family in a Changing Society* (New York: Free Press, 1980), p. 411.
2. Gerald R. Leslie and Elizabeth Leslie, *Marriage in a Changing World* (New York: John Wiley & Sons, 1980), p. 338.
3. Elizabeth Kübler-Ross, *On Death and Dying* (New York: Macmillan Publishing Company, Inc., 1969).
4. Reva S. Wiseman, "Crisis Theory and the Process of Divorce," Henslin, ed., *Marriage and Family*, pp. 429-437.
5. *You Can Ease the Hurt of Divorce* (Grand Rapids: Baker Book House, 1978), p. 4.
6. Charles R. Swindoll, *Strike the Original Match* (Portland, OR: Multnomah Press, 1980), pp. 141-148.
7. Jay E. Adams, *Marriage, Divorce and Remarriage in the Bible* (Phillipsburg, NJ: Presbyterian and Reformed Publishing Co., 1980).
8. Ibid., p. 24.
9. Ibid., p. 25.
10. Ibid., p. 95.

Seven

Alcohol

In many respects, alcohol is America's number one problem. Consider the following: There are 110 million drinkers in America. Ten percent of them are defined as alcoholics—that's 11 million people. Alcohol is the third largest killer of people in the United States—heart disease is first, then cancer, then alcohol. The person who is a problem alcoholic has only a 50 percent chance of reaching age fifty-one. The average life expectancy of a person who is a problem drinker is twelve years shorter than that of his friend who does not drink. One-half of all the fatal accidents on the highway are alcohol-related.[1] About fifty-six thousand people die on American highways each year and approximately twenty-eight thousand deaths are alcohol-related. A member of the San Diego Police Department told me recently that only one out of every two thousand people under the influence of alcohol is arrested, so a great majority are driving a lethal weapon under the influence and are never caught. They are eventually often involved in accidents. Each year we spend $15 billion just to pay the bills for alcohol: lost time at work, damage to property, and medical costs. For every fifteen people addicted to alcohol, there is only one addicted to heroin. We have a major national problem.

What then should be the response of the believer? What should be our attitude toward alcohol?

The Christian Attitude

I would like to suggest that there are three possible Christian options. Option number one is that you understand alcohol to be sinful and evil in and of itself, and therefore you have nothing to do with it. Option number two is that you understand alcohol to be a gift that can be abused, and therefore you must be very cautious about using it. Many European Christians obviously feel that way. In Germany and in France you will find beer and wine on the tables of evangelicals, some of whom are our missionaries or other leading evangelicals. They feel that it is a gift from God but that it must be used wisely.

There is a third option, however, which to my mind is the most helpful Christian option. I would like to suggest that we freely choose to abstain from the use of alcohol. The reason I propose this is that the use of alcohol in moderation is not specifically condemned, in and of itself, in the Word of God. But in our kind of situation, in a society in which alcohol has become such a major problem, I would like to see the believer say, "As for me and my house, we are going to draw the line and say no." I would like to see us do this not because drinking an occasional glass of wine in private is sinful but because our influence and our testimony for God is so important that we wouldn't want to offend a weaker brother who couldn't handle alcohol.

The Apostle Paul said that "if what I eat causes my brother to fall into sin, I will never eat meat again" (1 Cor. 8:13). It is not that it would be offensive for Paul himself, because for him eating meat was a neutral matter. But he said, "Some people have weak consciences. If they see me eating meat offered to idols, they will then be emboldened or encouraged to partake." So he said, "Therefore I am going to draw the line on something that is neutral but can have a negative influence. That is not legalism, that is not law, that is a conviction that I have come to."

I encourage you to carefully consider your own convictions and, before God and with fellow believers, to say, "How is my statement as a child of God to be most meaningful and sensitive to the world around me?" As for me and my house, we say no. I trust that before God you will make your own decision. That is where we all stand—before Him. In freedom, do the loving thing.

Bob Bartosch is a friend of mine. He grew up, went to a Baptist church in the Los Angeles area, graduated from Bob Jones University, pastored two Baptist churches, and eventually became an alcoholic. He took his first drink at the age of twenty-four, and then he discovered he could not control himself. He went into the secular business world. One day, by the grace of God and through the encouragement of Alcoholics Anonymous, he went dry. The day was October 15, 1973. Bob shared with me that he got so excited about his new life "dry" that he went back to school and earned a master's degree in alcohol counseling. Today he is the director of the Long Beach Council on Alcoholism and has had the privilege of influencing others both as a believer and as a reformed alcoholic.

Bob has encouraged me by providing me with all kinds of literature on alcoholism. I don't have any alcoholics among my relatives, and Bob has been helpful by introducing me to people who understand what alcoholism is all about. Bob says that for the evangelical who starts to drink, the problem is far greater than for anybody else in our society. One out of ten drinkers in the general population becomes an alcoholic. But one out of two drinkers who come from an evangelical home becomes an alcoholic. At a women's retreat of the Baptist General Conference two years ago in one of the cabins, one of the ladies said, "I think my husband is an alcoholic." There were eight women in the room, and four of them said they had a similar situation in their home—a husband, a child, a family member. The minute we begin to examine this problem we discover that it touches many evangelical families. Many people are touched by it—a daughter, a son, a mate, a parent, a cousin— perhaps someone in your family. Therefore, it is not a matter of indifference.

What should be our attitude toward alcoholism? Some say, "Ignore it. It will go away." But it won't. It is here. It is real. Others say, "You ought to preach against it." But that may be an unfortunate attitude toward it also, because when people are scolded they are not as likely to be healed as when they are loved. There is a common feeling abroad that if we don't go home from church feeling that we have been whipped, we haven't really been to church. I am not of that persuasion. I am not convinced that if you go home feeling whipped you have therefore had a good experience. There are other ways to become Christlike. So I am not going to whip the alcoholic.

There is a third option. The redemptive community must reach out and say, "All of us may not have that problem, but we want you to know that we are all sinners in need of God's grace. If alcohol is your problem, we want you to know that God cares for you and loves you—and so do we. We want to encourage you and help restore you to health."

The Afflicted

Philip Hanson has written a book that I commend to you. It is called *Sick and Tired of Being Sick and Tired.*[2] Hanson is an ordained Lutheran clergyman, an evangelical who directs alcohol rehabilitation at the Northwestern Hospital in Minneapolis. It is his conviction that the prodigal son in Luke 15 was an alcoholic. He says there are symptoms in the prodigal's life-style that suggest he was addicted to alcohol.

I don't happen to share that conviction. I don't think the text really tells us that. But the story of the prodigal son, in his relationship with his father and his family, illustrates principles that are helpful in dealing with any major sin in your life. It certainly applies to alcoholism.

The prodigal son was an afflicted person. He said, " 'Father, give me my share of the estate.' So

[his father] divided his property between them."
Then the son left (Luke 15:12).

What we have here is a son who is caught up in self-centered living. He wants comfort, he wants to be on his own, he wants to enjoy his freedom. The father realizes at this point that it is probably too late to say, "No, son, you can't have your share." He says, "All right; go. Here it is." Hanson reminds us that the alcoholic, like the prodigal, is caught up in self-centered living. He wants comfort. He wants to round off the rough edges of life and make them a little more bearable.

The disease

Maybe at the bottom of that glass or bottle is the elixir that will enable the alcoholic to handle the pressures of life. An alcoholic is one who has a lack or loss of control when it comes to alcohol. The alcoholic is one who cannot in fact choose whether he will drink or not. Once he has taken a drink he can no longer predict his future behavior. Drunkenness is sin, but it also can become so addictive that it is like a disease.

Colleen Wellborn died about a year ago. I remember the day she came into my office. She had just been released from prison. She had been in prison for the third time because of drunk driving. Colleen was a mere wisp of a lady weighing about ninety pounds. She had heart trouble and cancer. But she came to know the Lord and her life opened up to Him. She used to sit right down in front in church. She hung on every word. She opened her Bible and read it. She had devotions, she attended church Sunday morning, Sunday evening, Wednesday night. She related herself to the people of the church, and they loved her and she loved them. But on three different occasions I was called to her home and she was as drunk as a person could be. Sobbing through her tears she said, "Pray for me, pastor. I can't control it." Twice she tried to commit suicide. I still remember the day I went to her house and the blood was streaming down her arm. She was drunk again, and she said, "I just can't go on. The problem is bigger than I can handle. Pray for me." We prayed together—and God graciously took her to Himself.

I thought, here was a woman who wanted as best she knew how to follow the Lord, as best she knew how to have victory over alcohol—but she was controlled by it. She would make victorious strides for weeks and months, but the minute she got close to alcohol she was right back in the center of her problem again. The alcoholic cannot touch alcohol. The alcoholic says, "Once you're dry you either stay dry or you get drunk again."

The deliverance

What is the way to deliverance? *First, you almost have to "bottom out."* "After he had spent everything, there was a severe famine in that whole country, and he began to be in need. So he went and hired himself out to a citizen of that country, who sent him to his fields to feed pigs. He longed to fill his stomach with the pods that the pigs were eating, but no one gave him anything" (Luke 15:14-16). That was the height of ignominy for a Jew—slopping pigs, feeding dirty, unclean animals. Suddenly, he hit the bottom with a thud.

Sometimes the alcoholic does that and wakes up in a hospital bed. Or he wakes up in a jail cell, drying out in a holding tank. Or he is at the side of his bed with his head in his hands at two in the morning, and his head is throbbing, and he says, "What have I done with my life?" Or in the middle of the night she may get up sobbing. Almost without control she may say, "I don't know where it is all going. I am just not in control." Alcohol has a way of taking a grip on somebody, and he hits bottom. It doesn't matter really whether it is alcoholism or lust-aholism, or dishonesty. You name the problem. It is only when you hit bottom that you have the potential to make strides toward physical and spiritual health.

Second, you must acknowledge your need. "When he came to his senses, he said, 'How many of my father's hired men have food to spare, and here I am starving to death!' " (Luke 15:17). Suddenly he says, "What am I doing here?" The first step in Alcoholics Anonymous's Twelve Steps is this: "We admitted that we were powerless over alcohol, that our lives had become unmanageable."[3] When you reach powerlessness and you realize that your problem is something you cannot control by yourself and you need to turn outside of yourself for help, you are on your way home. If you tell someone with a problem to read a book or go to a seminar or listen to the pastor or listen to someone else's advice, he can go and listen and hear and never change unless he comes to this conviction: "I want to change." God can change anybody, but He is dependent on the response of our will. We can choose not to be changed, or we can allow Him to change us if we desire it.

Third, you must seek help. " 'I will set out and go back to my father and say to him: Father, I have sinned against heaven and against you. I am no longer worthy to be called your son; make me like one of your hired men.' So he got up and went to his father" (Luke 15:18-20). That is where hope is, that is where healing is—in the presence of the Father. The rewards of the Christian life are offered to those who surrender and admit that they cannot help themselves, that they need Him desperately, that they need His provision and His grace.

God has not only offered Himself. He also offers the Body of Christ. He offers Christian counselors. An organization that I recommend to you is Alcoholics Anonymous. Since that organization started in 1935, one million people have gone dry through its encouragement.[4] Eighty-five percent of all the people who are healed of alcoholism are healed through the agency and the help of Alcoholics Anonymous. In addition, 12 percent are healed through conversion. Only 3 percent ever overcome alcohol unless they are converted or are healed through Alcoholics Anonymous. A combination of meeting the Lord and attending Alcoholics Anonymous is better still.

The grace of our God and redemption through Christ and the assistance of an organization like Alcoholics Anonymous is a healing combination that God has raised up in our day. One out of every two people who go to their first Alcoholics Anonymous meeting will never again take a drink. Twenty-five percent will struggle off and on and finally get victory. Twenty-five percent do not stay with the program.[5] Alcoholics Anonymous is an agency that I believe God has raised up as an ally of the Church. Add faith in the Lord, and you have an unbeatable combination.

The Affected

Alcoholics Anonymous's Twelve Steps are extraordinary. They are almost like a course in discipleship. I have those Twelve Steps[6] all written out with verses attached to each one. They are almost like a manual on maturity in Christ, a helpful program that our God has provided for the afflicted.

But what about those who are affected? Sometimes the alcoholic's family goes through as much pain as the alcoholic himself. You see it in the prodigal son's older brother. The young son comes home, the father welcomes him—and the older son is really upset. Can't you just hear him pouting? "I have been working hard around here. I have given my life to you, and I have helped you, and this young kid comes home and you throw a banquet." So he wallows in self-pity, in jealousy, in bitterness.

Often the family of the alcoholic does the same thing. They say, "Look, we have put up with this for a long time. We have kept our lives straight. We have cared for each other. But you—you have gone off and wasted your life and spent your money, and you come sobbing back home to us." Such a family is like the elder brother: sometimes not helpful at all. If anything, they are resentful and bitter.

But the healing family is represented by the father. The prodigal son went to his father. "But while he was still a long way off, his father saw him and was filled with compassion for him; he ran to his son, threw his arms around him and kissed him. The son said to him, 'Father, I have sinned against heaven and against you' " (Luke 15:20-21). Can you see the picture? The father goes to bed each night and lifts up his eyes to the Lord and says, "Father, God, watch over my boy. Bring him home." And the next day he goes out to the road and he looks down it—day after day, night and day—and seemingly there is no hope. But he keeps praying and keeps looking, he keeps waiting and waiting and waiting, and one day there is a spot on the horizon, and the spot gets larger and becomes visible as a person, and then the father realizes it is his boy. That old heart begins to thump, and he runs and meets that young son and throws his arms around him and kisses him and says, "Boy, it is good to have you home!" It is a picture of the waiting father.

You will discover when you make your move toward God that God is running toward you. That is the nature of His grace. It is the nature of His care. His grace is always greater than our sin, and He is there to heal, to forgive, to make whole, to restore. It is sometimes a tough thing for a family to continue to trust God and to believe that someday that dad, that mom, that mate, that child is going to come back home to experience victory over alcohol. It happens because there are people who continue to care, continue to pray, and continue to provide the redemptive community and setting in which healing can occur.

Where are you right now? You may be concerned about your own consumption of alcohol. You have discovered that you desperately need to take a drink at the end of the day. You can't quite handle pressure without it. Maybe you have to go off on your own and get an alcoholic lift. You may be on your way to a problem. You may already be in the problem.

We want you to know that you are loved. We want you to know that there is help. Will you claim those resources? If you are young, draw the line now—don't get started. It is not worth it. If you are not touched by the temptation to drink, let me encourage you not to become self-righteous. We are sinners—all of us. It may not be in the area of alcohol, it may be in our pride. All of us need His grace. All of us stand before Him needing what He has to offer. To all of you, and to myself, I would say, "May God enable us to be the kind of people who care enough, love enough, trust enough to let anyone in need be accepted and, by the grace of God, healed." We want to see people changed. We want that to happen in your life. Will you let God do it?

For Further Thought

1. How do you relate to alcoholics?

2. What is your attitude towards alcoholic consumption? Are you consciously biblical in your practice?

3. Is there hope for the alcoholic? Where do we find helpful resources?

4. What lessons are found in the story of the prodigal son?

Notes
1. Robert Bartosch, director of the Long Beach Council on Alcoholism, Long Beach, California.
2. Philip Hanson, *Sick and Tired of Being Sick and Tired* (Minneapolis: Park Printing Inc., 1971).
3. Duane Mehl, *You and the Alcoholic in Your Home* (Minneaplis: Augsburg Publishing House, 1979), p. 143.
4. *A Clergyman Asks About Alcoholics Anonymous*, rev. ed. (New York: A.A. World Services, Inc., 1979), p. 5.
5. Carol Oden, *Healing the Hopeless* (Pecos, NM: Dove Publications, 1974), p. 10.
6. Mehl, *You and the Alcoholic*, p. 143.

Eight

Loneliness

"O Lord, you have searched me and you know
me. You know when I sit and when I rise; you per-
ceive my thoughts from afar. You discern my going
out and my lying down; you are familiar with all
my ways. Before a word is on my tongue you know
it completely, O Lord. You hem me in, behind and
before; you have laid your hand upon me. Such
knowledge is too wonderful for me, too lofty for me
to attain. Where can I go from your Spirit? Where
can I flee from your presence? If I go up to the
heavens, you are there; if I make my bed in the
depths, you are there. If I rise on the wings of the
dawn, if I settle on the far side of the sea, even
there your hand will guide me, your right hand
will hold me fast" (Ps. 139:1-10).

Aloneness is a frightening, chilling, cold experience for the human spirit. T. S. Eliot has gone so
far as to suggest that hell is to be alone. There is
nothing to escape from and nothing to escape to.
"One," says Eliot, "is always alone."[1] Whether that

is literally true of hell or not, anybody who has been alone knows the hellishness of loneliness. It eats away and tears away at the human spirit.

Three psychiatrists in a symposium—Rosenbaum, Sheiners and Winkhart—agree that loneliness is perhaps the most dangerous and widespread illness of our day. They go on to add, "It has reached epidemic proportions in America." Rosenbaum himself then adds, "Seventy-five to 90 percent of adult Americans experience chronic loneliness,"[2] to which Norman Cousins answers, "All man's history is an endeavor to shatter his loneliness."[3] Too pessimistic? Perhaps. But listen to a contemporary writer: "Loneliness is discovering that your parents are getting a divorce and you are being torn by a pull toward each parent. Loneliness is hearing the umpire call, 'Strike three; you're out'—when the winning run is on third base. Loneliness is a college freshman who is glad to be away from home but who feels empty on the first day of classes. Loneliness is a six-year-old who does not know the name of any other first-graders. Loneliness is a mother whose children are all away at school. Loneliness is going to a party with friends and finding only chit-chat and the small talk of dangling conversation. Loneliness is lying in a hospital bed looking at the ceiling and asking, 'How long? How long?' Loneliness is saying 'no' when all other girls say 'yes.' Loneliness is realizing that in some ways you can never go home again."[4]

Causes of Loneliness

What causes loneliness? Let me suggest five reasons.

The first is guilt. Jacob defrauded his brother Esau of his birthright and then fled. Jacob went through twenty lonely years struggling with the guilt of his own deceitfulness, and then after a very nervous reunion, his loneliness left. Guilt produces loneliness. (See Gen. 27:1-29; 33:1-17.)

The second is betrayal. Hosea the prophet was married to Gomer. The marriage seems to have started normally enough. They apparently had a good marriage for a time. They had their own child. And then her eyes began to wander, and lust began to fill her spirit. She began to leave her home and flee from her commitment to her husband Hosea. Gomer became a woman of the street and had two children by other men. In that deep emptiness of his spirit we sense that Hosea, a betrayed man, was lonely. (See Hos. 1.)

The third is grief. Lazarus dies, and Mary and Martha, devoted sisters of Lazarus, are going through the process of grief. Jesus arrives four days after the death. One at a time, the sisters both say the same thing: "If you had been here, it would not have happened." (See John 11:17-32.) Emptiness comes to them because one who had been by their side has been wrenched from them, and they feel the vacuum of Lazarus's departure. They are going through the grieving process, and they are lonely. Grief causes loneliness.

My dad died a couple of years ago, but my mother has done quite well. She was eighty-one last summer. She gets out and visits and shares her life and is very active. And yet on occasion my phone rings late at night, and there is Mom at the other end of the line. I know what she is going through. Her company has left, the meeting is

over, the condominium is empty—and she is still
going through the grieving process. She is lonely.
When you have shared your life with one man for
fifty-one years and have walked and talked and
cried and laughed together, and now you are
alone, you grieve.

The fourth is insecurity. We live in a very com-
petitive world. When we don't do well, we feel
lonely. As a child and as a young person, I
attended a little church in Wisconsin during the
summertime—First Baptist Church in Sister Bay,
Wisconsin. The town's population was 429, the
church had 200 in attendance. Once a month on
Sunday evenings we would have a musical. A lot of
the local people played instruments and sang. One
Sunday night I was to play a marimba solo. I
played a marimba as a young person—not well,
but courageously. That Sunday evening I was to
play "Ring the Bells of Heaven." I practiced it and I
knew it well, so I left my music at home. I stood up,
played the first line, and then my memory failed
me. I played the first line a second time. Four
times I played the first line of "Ring the Bells of
Heaven." I put my mallets on the marimba and sat
down. There were 200 people there, but I was
alone.

Have you ever played some of those solos? Do
you remember when you were on the line for something and you did not perform as you wish you
could have? Do you remember how lonely you felt?
In a performance-oriented society, any time we
don't do well we feel like we are standing alone and
everybody is pointing a finger at us. Insecurity
makes us lonely.

The fifth is isolation. Elijah enjoys a great triumph on Mount Carmel, and all of Israel rises up and prays to God, and the prophets of Baal are slain. It's a great victory for faith and for God. But the next day, pursued by Jezebel, Elijah in the wilderness cries out, "I and I alone am left. I am the only one that has not bowed the knee." (See 1 Kings 19:1-18.) In his loneliness you sense the deep loneliness of God's man. Isolation brings loneliness.

One Valentine's Day we received a card here at church, attractively done: "To Jesus or whomever else would like to read that which is herein: O, Lord, I am so wounded. I feel like I have been crushed by the multitudes. They step on me, yet they don't know it. O Father, I know they don't wish to hurt me, but they are trying to help me; but I am unnoticed. They hear me but turn away. I am forsaken in your people's actions toward me. They know this not, Lord. Help me to find one who will care, understand, but not judge. O, Father, I thank you for helping me when I need you as you have helped this wonderful church. Father, this is a great place to grow and learn your ways, but I cannot find my place here, Lord."

I hurt with that individual. I sense that, in the midst of hundreds of people, that individual is an island. Maybe you wrote that letter, or maybe you could have written that letter. Today you know what it is to be alone. You are a loner in the midst of many others, and you hurt.

Cure for Loneliness

How do we deal with loneliness? Some people can't, and so they go to great extremes as they become immobilized. Who can ever forget that final line written by Edward Arlington Robinson in his poem "Richard Cory"? All the accomplishments of Richard Cory are described, and then one night he "went home and put a bullet through his head."⁵ Some people simply cannot cope, and so they take their own lives. Others become frantically active. They become workaholics, or alcoholics, or sexually promiscuous—all attempts to overcome loneliness.

There is a better way. I would like to suggest biblical directives in curing the sickness of loneliness.

A healthy self-esteem

The first cure is a healthy self-esteem that comes from an understanding of who we are in God's eyes. You have to know who you are as a person in Christ. I am not talking about narcissism. I am not talking about the ego-tripping of people who surround themselves with mirrors. I am concerned when Robert Schuller writes a book called *Self-Esteem, the New Reformation,* which seems to suggest that the controlling motif in a Christian's life is self-esteem. You start not with self but with God.

Self-esteem, however, when properly understood, is a genuinely biblical concept. You are to love your neighbor as yourself, said Jesus. The Bible assumes that you must have a healthy view of self to have a healthy view of your neighbor. If you don't have a healthy view of yourself, you will have an unhealthy view of your neighbor.

Romans 12 says that you are to give yourself as a living sacrifice to God, which is your reasonable service. Then it says, "Think soberly" (v. 3). Understand yourself as you really are. How do you do that? You can build your understanding on the shifting sands of your own performance and people's opinions, or you can build it on the bedrock of what God says about you. What does He say about you? (1) He says you are worthy. We are all worthy because we are His creation. Believer and unbeliever are made by Him, and we are the handiwork of our God. His image in us has been besmirched by sin, but indelibly built into all of us is the fact that we are all His creation and, therefore, we are worthy. (2) He says you are competent. God has given gifts to all of His people, and we are all competent. Different people have different gifts, but all are gifted by Him. No one is left out. (3) He says you are secure. "Who shall separate us from the love of Christ? Shall trouble or hardship or persecution or famine or nakedness or danger or sword? . . . No, in all these things we are more than conquerors through him who loved us." Nothing can "separate us from the love of God that is in Christ Jesus our Lord" (Rom. 8:35-37,39). That is security! (4) He says you are loved. If John 3:16 says anything, it says that God loves His world and does not look at us abstractly but looks at us compassionately. He loves us unconditionally. He loves you as you are.

When you begin to understand who you are in His eyes and what He says about you, you begin to understand and accept yourself as a person of great worth. God through Christ has made you worthwhile—not in and of yourself, but through His grace. Once you begin to understand who you are, then you can begin to accept the fact that you must accept yourself.

A healthy relationship to God

The second cure is a healthy relationship to God. Psalm 139:1-6 tells us that He knows us. He has searched us. He knows when I sit and when I rise; He knows my thoughts, my going out, my lying down. He is familiar with all my ways. The psalmist says, "Such knowledge is too wonderful for me." Do you know what that means? Every thought you have had this morning is known by God. Everything you have done this week He knows. Everything you are anticipating this next week He knows. He knows us entirely. We are an open book. We have been laid bare before Him.

The psalmist talks about God's knowledge of us in a variety of ways. I sit, and He knows. I stand, and He knows. I go, and He knows. I think, and He knows it. I am known entirely. Not only am I known, but also He is with me. He knows me and still loves me. "Where can I go from your Spirit? Where can I flee from your presence? If I go up to the heavens, you are there; if I make my bed in the depths, you are there. If I rise on the wings of the dawn, if I settle on the far side of the sea," I can't go anyplace where you are not (vv. 7-10). You can't take a trip away from Him. You can't hide from Him. "Where can I go from your Spirit?" God is saying, "I will never leave you nor forsake you." That is His assurance. There may be times when you say, "Nobody else cares. Nobody else understands." But God does! In all of your life as a believer, you cannot escape from His presence and His care. He is there.

Let me read again from the letter I received that was addressed to Jesus: "Lord, you have done more for me than anyone ever tried to think or care about doing. More so even than my parents. Thank you, Lord, for being there when I have no one to cry to or talk to by mail or by phone. I know you care. I love you for that. Lord, you are already my valentine for life and forever, but just for the sake of asking, please be mine, Jesus. I am yours. We are each other's always." I am grateful that the writer of the letter has found in the Lord a strength that is in Him alone. The psalmist is saying that a relationship with God, a God who cares, is the basic way to deal with loneliness. We need Him.

Such a relationship takes place when you receive Him into your life. If you have ever come to the place where you have been lonely but have never received Him, that is where you must begin. That is the first step. As Augustine said, "Thou madest us for Thyself, and our heart is restless until it repose in Thee." The vacuum, the emptiness you feel in your life, can be filled only by the God who created it. He made us for fellowship, and you need it. So He offers Himself, and so you receive Him by faith. You become His child. You can do that now. You don't have to wait for a special event. You can do it right now by reaching out and saying, "Lord Jesus, I am here. I am lonely. I need you as Saviour and friend. I confess that. I receive you into my life." Then take each day and say, "Lord, I need you today."

I don't know how you wake up in the morning. I doubt that you throw back the covers and sing, "Praise God from Whom all blessings flow." I doubt that you leap from bed and sing the Hallelujah Chorus. I have always felt that it is very difficult to be spiritual with morning mouth. You at least need to gargle to get the day started. But very early in the morning you can say, "Lord, I need you today. I need you and I give myself to you again." Commit each day afresh to God. "I don't know about tomorrow, but I need you today." Entrust it to His care. He wants to march with you through your day as your Friend.

A healthy relationship with people

The third cure is a healthy relationship with people. You see, we really do need God and people. Many have said to me, "Isn't it enough that we have the Lord?" My answer is yes and no—yes eternally, no temporarily. God made us for each other. Jesus needed people. In the loneliness of the garden He took along three of His closest friends—Peter, James and John—and He said, "I am going through great travail of soul, and I need you here." Unfortunately, they fell asleep when He needed them, but they knew—as you and I also discover—that as Jesus taught, as Jesus practiced, we need the Body of Christ. Paul knew it. At the end of 2 Timothy he talks about people who have departed, and so he says, "Timothy, come and see me." You can picture the plaintiveness of his cry: "Timothy, come and see me." We need people.

The letter I read earlier puts it this way: "Our church is a good church. I like the people, the sermons, even the landscaping. It is indeed a Christian land of splendor filled with praises, love, and diligent, faithful people. Why, O Lord, knowing this am I a loner amidst your flock? I am not looking for a trophy, a gold medal; I am just trying to find a group of a few people who I can be a genuine part of." Jesus knows how much we need each other. We were created for each other. We were created for the Body. Would you take the challenge to reach out—reach out to make friends?

I know a couple who has visited literally hundreds of churches through the years, in a ministry they have, and they say, "We have never yet found an unfriendly church." That says something about them. Everywhere they go, people are friendly because they are friendly. Those who care are cared for, and those who are uncaring often find that they are lonely. As you begin to reach out, as you begin to show an interest in people, you discover friends. The more you rehearse your problems and want everybody to minister to you, the more isolated you often become. But as you begin to reach out you discover that your friendliness is reciprocated. Reach out and begin to serve. As you begin to minister to the needs of others, the Lord begins to meet your needs. One of the best ways to deal with loneliness is to minister to people. My mom has been recently doing that. After all, when you are only eighty-one you have lots of strength left, so you might as well use it. So she makes hospital calls and she invites lonely people over to her house. She is discovering great strength in reaching out and ministering to others.

Are you lonely today? I trust that you will find people who are sensitive to your loneliness, who touch you, who minister to you. When I am lonely, I hope you will minister to me. We need each other.

Go back to Calvary. It is sometime between 12:00 noon and 3:00 and premature darkness has come like a heavy black cloak on that hill. The mid-afternoon air is split by the Aramaic words of the

Lord Jesus as He says, "Eloi, Eloi, lama sabach-thani?" "My God, my God, why have you forsaken me?" Jesus looks into the heavens, and the heavens are dumb. He listens for God's voice, but He hears nothing. Jesus in that hour knows what it is to be alone. He understands that. He understands your why's and your cries. He understands your pain, He understands what it is like to be alone. He offers His care, His understanding and His presence. He also offers you His family. Loneliness need not be chronic. Jesus came, Jesus died, and Jesus provides His family to meet us in moments of loneliness. Will you claim that provision?

For Further Thought

1. When do you feel most lonely?

2. How do you feel about yourself? Are you happy with your self-image? What could you change?

3. What kind of relationship do you have with God? Could it be improved? What next step do you have in mind?

Notes

1. Quoted by Elizabeth Skoglund, *Loneliness* (Downers Grove, IL: Inter-Varsity Press, 1975), p. 6.
2. B. W. Woods, *You Can Overcome Loneliness* (Grand Rapids: Baker Book House, 1978), p. 3.
3. Skoglund, *Loneliness*, p. 33.
4. Wade B. Hine. Quoted by Woods, *You Can Overcome*, pp. 3-4.
5. Walter Blair, Theodore Hornberger and Randall Stewart, eds., *The Literature of the United States*, vol. 2, rev. ed. (Chicago: Scott Foresman & Company, 1953), p. 890.

Nine

Guilt

Guilt is universal. It is one thing that you have in common with people around the world. Paul Tournier has said that "no man lives free of guilt."[1] Civilization always has within it the potential for guilt. Whenever you have standards, laws, and rules that govern a people, you have the potential for guilt. The greater the civilization, the more sophisticated it is, the more likelihood there is that guilt will be found among its people.

We would like to think that we are a civilized nation. We know at least this much: One of the marks of our civilization is that we know guilt. Knowing it, what do we do about it? If we deny it, then comes anxiety, anger, bitterness, and sometimes overt aggressiveness. These are some of the results of failing to deal with guilt. But those who deal with it have the potential for freedom, for the relaxation of internal pressure, for the restoration of wholesome and free relationships among people. Peace can be ours when we deal with guilt.

Guilt Triggered

Look at one man who experienced guilt on a number of occasions. In the story before us he begins to deal with guilt in a much healthier fashion than he had in the past. His name is King David.

In the first part of the story you see his *guilt triggered.* "The king said to Joab and the army commanders with him, 'Go throughout the tribes of Israel from Dan to Beersheba and enroll the fighting men, so that I may know how many there are.' But Joab replied to the king, 'May the Lord your God multiply the troops a hundred times over and may the eyes of my lord the king see it. But why does my lord the king want to do such a thing?' The king's word, however, overruled Joab and the army commanders; so they left the presence of the king to enroll the fighting men of Israel" (2 Sam. 24:2-4). David says, "Go. Count them." Joab says, "No. Why do you want to do that?" The king says, "Count them." So Joab goes out and counts them: "There were eight hundred thousand able-bodied men who could handle a sword, and in Judah five hundred thousand"—a total of 1,300,000 fighting men. "David was conscience-stricken after he had counted the fighting men, and he said to the Lord, 'I have sinned greatly in what I have done. Now, O Lord, I beg you, take away the guilt of your servant. I have done a very foolish thing' " (2 Sam. 24:10).

Notice the anatomy of guilt. The first element is that there is a norm or standard. God says, "Trust me. Rely on me. I will be your resource for victory." In the past it really didn't matter how many soldiers the nation had. If God was with them, the victory belonged to the people of God, and so all along the way God's people had been instructed, "Trust me. I am your King. I am your Lord. You can trust me to give the victory, but you must walk humbly with me and trust me."

The second element in the anatomy of guilt is *pride*. David turns to numbers and resources. Keil and Delitzsch in their commentary on this text say, David had a "thirst for conquest which was the motive for the undertaking . . . self-exaltation . . . he sought for the strength and the glory of his kingdom in the number of the people and their readiness for war."[2] God says, "Trust me." David places his trust in men and in numbers, and he lifts himself up in pride and self-confidence rather than humbling himself by trusting in God. The norm: "Trust me." David ignores the norm. He trusts in his own pride.

The third element in the anatomy of guilt is an *emotional response*. He is "conscience-stricken." Inside he senses that he has failed to live up to God's standard. Breaking the divine standard arouses the sickening emotional response that we call "guilt." The dictionary defines *guilt* as "a feeling of blameworthiness for having committed a crime or a wrong." It is "a feeling of failure," says Stein.

I have come to the conclusion that there are two basic types of guilt. The first is psychological in nature, while the second tends to be moral in nature. The two can be one and the same, but for purposes of analysis let's distinguish them. Bruce Narramore and Bill Counts, in a book called *Guilt and Freedom*, say that psychological guilt includes "internal fear of punishment, a sense of unworthiness, or a fear of alienation and rejection."[3] As you apply those concepts to your moral life, it would seem that guilt understood morally has two pluses. The first is that guilt is a reminder of our need. When you feel guilty, you are reminded that you have a need in your life. One of the great problems with leprosy is that the leper loses his sensitivity. People who have leprosy don't have feeling in their feet, and therefore they stub their toes and damage their feet. There is no pain sensor sending out a message saying, "Don't do that." Pain is a reminder of need. One of the helpful things about pain is that it forces you to do something about it.

The second plus is that guilt becomes a motivator for change. When you feel guilt, you are motivated to resolve it and to get rid of the pressure. When you feel that your life is getting out of joint because of guilt, you want to do something to bring your life back into line.

What is the role of conscience? David was conscience-stricken. What is conscience? Huckleberry Finn said that conscience takes up more room than all the rest of a person's insides. Do you ever feel that way? Do you ever sense that the largest organ in your body is your conscience?

Some say that conscience is an executioner, that it is bent on our destruction, that it gnaws away at us. Some would have us to believe that it is an island of purity in a sea of guilt. Conscience is the one pure thing in us. We are a large mass of guilt, and conscience is the pure island within it. Conscience stands inside a person and reminds him that there is wholeness in the midst of brokenness.

There is a better answer. Your conscience is the custodian of your highest values. Your conscience reminds you when you don't live up to those values. As a Christian your values become informed, monitored, and instructed by the Holy Spirit. If a person is walking with the Lord, conscience is a valuable tool when it is instructed by his Christian value system. When you fail to live up to your highest values your conscience says, "This is the will of God. This is the holiness of God. This is the way of God." Your conscience becomes a custodian of those values if it is allowed to be taught and informed by the Holy Spirit.

Guilt Acknowledged

"David was conscience-stricken after he had counted the fighting men, and he said to the Lord, 'I have sinned greatly in what I have done. Now, O Lord, I beg you, take away the guilt of your servant. I have done a very foolish thing' " (2 Sam. 24:10). How much healthier is this response than David's earlier responses to his own sin!

There are all kinds of ways in which you can deny or get rid of guilt.

The repressive tactic

You can dodge guilt. You can use all kinds of tactics and devices to avoid it. David used one back in 2 Samuel 11. One day he was outside and saw a lovely lady taking a bath. He noticed her, and his eyes lingered over her, and he lusted after her, and he wanted her.

So he sent a servant to get Bathsheba. When she arrived, he made love to her. Later, they discovered that she was pregnant. David now had a big problem because Bathsheba's husband was off to war and it would look like she had done something amiss. So David recalled Uriah to come back from the war. He assumed that Uriah would go home and sleep with his lovely wife, and then everybody would say, "Ah, Bathsheba is going to have a child. It happened during furlough."

But Uriah didn't go home. David was upset and said to Uriah, "Why didn't you go home to your wife?" Uriah said, "When my fellow soldiers are all out there fighting the battle, why should I be home enjoying my wife?" So David got Uriah drunk, thinking that when he was drunk he would go home to her, but still he refused. David now saw no other option but to send Uriah to the front lines, where he was killed.

David chose to repress his guilt rather than to deal with it. He hid the evidence of it. If you don't want to deal with guilt frontally, you deny it. You repress it.

The rebellious tactic

People sometimes refuse to accept fault. It is someone else's fault, not mine. I'm not the cause. It's "society," it's my "lousy home," it's the kind of "job" I have. We blame everything on our job, our home, on someone else. We are rebellious.

Think about the Garden of Eden. Adam is created, and then Eve. These two lovely people enjoy life—but they are told, "There is one tree—you must not eat from that tree." One day Eve is in the garden, and the snake meets her. They converse back and forth, and Satan speaks through the snake and says, "Try the tree." Eve says, "We don't eat from that tree." The snake says, "God knows that the moment you eat from that tree you will be able to discern good from evil." And Eve feels a little cheated. "God is keeping some good things from us," she thinks. So she takes from the tree and eats it. She then says to Adam, "You know, we haven't had any fruit salad around the house lately. How about some fruit from the tree?" And he also takes some of the fruit. (See Gen. 3:1-12.)

Now the two of them feel guilty, so they hide. God comes into the garden and says, "Adam, where are you?" From his hiding place in the bushes Adam says, "We're over here." He feels embarrassed, and God begins to deal with the sin of Adam and Eve. Adam then becomes rebellious. He says, "The woman you put here with me . . ." He put the guilt on Eve and even pushed it one step further: "The woman YOU put here"—as if God were responsible for setting a trap for him. Rebellious people try to skirt guilt by laying it on others rather than dealing with it personally.

The recessive tactic

This tactic is the self-accusatory tendency to feel that when anything goes wrong it must be my fault. If something goes wrong at work, "It must be me!" If something goes wrong in the house, "It must be me!"

In Dostoevsky's great novel, *The Brothers Karamazov*, every brother admits to the murder of his father except the one brother who did it. All of us tend to feel that when something goes wrong, we are guilty. One day when Jesus met with His disciples He said, "One of you will deny me." Their response was incredible. They all began to ask, "Is it I?" They knew their own human hearts well enough to realize that they were all potentially capable of denying Christ, and so they all accepted the potential guilt for that denial.

Carl Michaelson says that there is a difference between dogs and cats. He says that dogs are recessive personalities. When a dog does something wrong, you talk to it and it admits guilt. In fact, it will admit guilt even when it is innocent.[5] When we moved to San Diego, we had a dog. She didn't adjust well to the move. She had become acclimated to her previous home, but her new home made her nervous. So she became anxious and, in the process, began not only to eat food but also to eat the house. She gnawed at our doorpost and tried to eat her way through some screens. We would come home and find wood splinters on the floor near the doorpost and the minute we looked at her she would flatten herself out. She would put her tail between her legs because she felt guilty.

The point is this: The psychologist says that a dog accepts guilt but a cat doesn't. When a cat does something wrong you can look it right in the eye, but it will never admit guilt; it is the vindictive type. It will simply look right back at you. A cat apparently has no conscience.

Most people are like dogs, not like cats. Rather than dealing with their personal guilt they want to accept the guilt of others as well, and they overload their systems with self-accusation. "If something is wrong, it must be my fault," they say—and that attitude is also a device to deny personal guilt.

The rationalist tactic

The rationalist says, "Others do worse, you know." Or the classic statement: "That's just me, that's just the way I am"—which is supposed to cover everything. If you understand them, you understand their problem. They rationalize it away.

Judas did that when he betrayed our Lord. Judas may have come to the conclusion that Jesus was not the Messiah he looked for, the Messiah who would sit in power on King David's throne and bring peace and prosperity and defeat Rome. As he looked at Jesus, Judas began to have doubts about the possibility that He was the promised Messiah. It didn't look like He was going to a throne. It looked, rather, like He was going to a cross. Judas may have reasoned that he was doing Jesus a service because He was wrong. When people commit guilt-producing acts, they often rationalize them.

Guilt Solved

How do you solve the problem of guilt?

Discern its source

Where did that guilt come from? Is it of man? Is it of Satan? Or is it truly of God? One day the disciples were walking along and saw a blind man. They said to Jesus, "Who sinned, this man or his parents?" Jesus said, "Neither." The disciples wanted to lay human guilt on him—"The reason you are blind is that you have sinned, and God has judged your sin by making you blind." Jesus said, "Not true." If the disciples had been alone with that man they might have said, "When did you sin?" The man might have felt guilty about that, as much as to say, "Maybe they are right."

People live under the pressure of human guilt.

Sometimes husbands pressure wives, and sometimes wives pressure husbands. The process is often quite irrational. Often the will of God is not in it. Possessiveness or manipulation or desire for power is often the source of guilt. Such guilt is not worthy of cleansing and forgiveness, because there may be no sin at all involved in it.

Discern the source of the guilt that you feel. Is it simply from people or is it from God? I believe that Satan also brings on guilt. He is the angel of light. He is the "accuser of our brothers," as we are told in Revelation 12:10. Satan delights in making people feel guilty and laying burdens on them that are not from God.

Discern the source of guilt. David did: "Against you, you only, have I sinned" (Ps. 51:4). David knew that he stood before a holy God and that the guilt he carried was because he had offended a holy God who had called him to a life of obedience and purity. His guilt was legitimate, not contrived.

Accept proper responsibility

If it is sin against God, then accept the responsibility for it. If you haven't sinned against God, you don't have to accept responsibility before God for what you haven't done. If you have sinned against someone else, accept the responsibility for that. If you sin against yourself, admit that as well. Place the blame where it belongs. Accept proper responsibility.

Claim the victory

If you are dealing with guilt, perhaps the best trip you could take would be back to Mount Calvary. Look into the face of the crucified Christ who hung on a Roman cross, because on that cross were nailed your sin and your guilt. He bore them to the cross for you. That is why Paul could write in Romans 8:1: "Therefore, there is now no condemnation for those who are in Christ Jesus." He took your sin and your guilt, and He asks you to claim the victory.

God uses His Word and your conscience, however, to remind you that fellowship can still be broken. The guilt question has been covered at Calvary, but broken fellowship can still be caused by sin. David says in Psalm 51:12, "Restore to me the joy of your salvation." In his sin he did not lose salvation, which is always a gift of God's grace. What he lost was the freshness, the intimacy, the joy, the power, the beauty of an unbroken relationship. He was still a son, but he was afar off.

If you carry guilt because there is unconfessed sin in your life, listen to David: "Lord, cleanse me. Create in me a clean heart." First John 1:9 says, "If we confess our sins, he is faithful and just and will forgive us our sins and purify us from all unrighteousness." He wants to lift your guilt.

I have always been impressed by the attitude of the father in the parable of the prodigal son. The son sins and then returns home. While he is still some distance away, the father runs to meet him with outstretched arms. If you are carrying a load of guilt, turn to the Father. As soon as you turn, you will discover that He is running to you to put His outstretched arms around you and say, "I love you. Through my Son I provided the means of handling all your guilt. I want to restore you. I love you. Come home."

God's answer to human guilt is the way of the

cross, and the price has been paid. It is for you. It is the way of peace. Claim the victory.

For Further Thought

1. Guilt is a troublesome thing. Do you have some of it in your life?

2. Why do you think you feel guilty? What is the source?

3. Are you dealing with your guilt in a realistic fashion? What are you doing?

4. Have you claimed Christ's victory over your guilt? You could.

Notes
1. Paul Tournier, *Guilt and Grace: A Psychological Study* (New York: Harper & Row Publishers, Inc., 1962), p. 152.
2. Carl F. Kiel and Franz Delitzsch, *The Books of Samuel* (Grand Rapids: Wm. B. Eerdmans Publishing Co., 1960), p. 502.
3. Bruce Narramore and Bill Counts, *Guilt and Freedom* (Ventura, CA: Vision House, 1974), p. 19.
4. Carl Michaelson, *Faith for Personal Crises* (New York: Charles Scribner's Sons, 1958), pp. 42-43.
5. Ibid., p. 43.

Ten

Grief

"One day when Job's sons and daughters were feasting and drinking wine at the oldest brother's house, a messenger came to Job and said, 'The oxen were plowing and the donkeys were grazing nearby, and the Sabeans attacked and carried them off. They put the servants to the sword, and I am the only one who has escaped to tell you!'

"While he was still speaking, another messenger came and said, 'The fire of God fell from the sky and burned up the sheep and the servants, and I am the only one who has escaped to tell you!'

"While he was still speaking, another messenger came and said, 'The Chaldeans formed three raiding parties and swept down on your camels and carried them off. They put the servants to the sword, and I am the only one who has escaped to tell you!'

"While he was still speaking, yet another messenger came and said, 'Your sons and daughters were feasting and drinking wine at the oldest brother's house, when suddenly a mighty wind swept in from the desert and struck the four corners of the house. It collapsed on them and they are dead, and I am the only one who has escaped to tell you!' " (Job 1:13-19).

In Isaiah 53 we read that the Lord Jesus is a "man of sorrows and acquainted with grief." You have but to march through the pages of the New Testament in the Gospel account to discover that it is true. Jesus was a Man of Sorrows and acquainted with grief. He carried great burdens in His heart. By the same token, at certain points in life all of God's people for whom Christ died can also say, "We are men and women of sorrows and we too are acquainted with grief." You don't have to invite grief. You don't have to seek it. Grief comes. Grief is an experience of deep privation when something cherished is taken from you.

Edgar Jackson in his book *For the Living* says, "Grief is a young widow who must seek a means to bring up her three children alone. Grief is the angry reaction of a man so filled with shock, uncertainty and confusion that he strikes out at the nearest person. Grief is a little old lady who goes to the funeral of a stranger and cries her eyes out there. She is weeping now for herself—for events she is sure will come and for which she is trying to prepare herself. Grief is a mother walking daily to a nearby cemetery to stand quietly and alone for a few moments before she goes on about the tasks of the day. She knows that part of her is in the cemetery just as part of her is in her daily work. Grief is the silent knife-like terror and sadness that comes a hundred times a day when you start to speak to someone who is no longer there.

Grief is the emptiness that comes when you eat alone after eating with another for many years. Grief is teaching yourself somehow to go to bed without saying 'goodnight' to the one who has died. Grief is the helpless wishing that things were different when you know that they are not and never will be again."[1]

In our study of coping with the unknown, we reminded you that Professor Holmes at the University of Washington said that "all grief has impact units."[2] The death of a spouse is the greatest of all traumas—100 impact units he gave it. Number five is the death of a close relative, the fifth most significant trauma you will face in your life. Both are grief experiences. Number two on the list is divorce, and that also is a grief experience. Anything once cherished and now gone causes a feeling of deep privation.

Grief comes in a variety of ways. Sometimes it comes very early. Sometimes a child experiences it. John Claypool in his book *Tracks of a Fellow Struggler* says that when he was four years old he had a puppy, a fat brown and white butterball named Jiggs. One day they were out playing in the backyard, frolicking about as puppies and little boys do. He went running inside and Jiggs was right behind him, as he did so the screen door slammed on Jiggs and broke his neck. He had a convulsion and died before his eyes. Years later, he said, "I can still remember the feeling of horror and unbelief."[3] For many of us grief did not come in our later years; it came very early in life—when something cherished was gone and we felt deep grief.

People handle grief very differently. Children

don't know how to handle it. They sometimes simply act out their feelings. They don't talk about it. They deal with it as best they know how. Sometimes middle-aged people change their life-styles when they respond to grief. If they have been active, all of a sudden they become quiet. If they have been quiet, suddenly they may become very active. The change is a response to grief that you can't handle any other way. For an older person, grief is sometimes accompanied by physical symptoms. If people are quiet and withdrawn by nature, grief may send them through a long quiet period.

The first funeral I conducted as a young pastor was for a little six-year-old girl struck while riding on a sled. Her mom and dad went through years of quiet grieving. They weren't very talkative by nature, and they managed their grief in a lonely, quiet fashion.

Other people are rather volatile, and they handle grief very differently. I conducted a funeral several years ago, and after I finished, people came up and looked into the casket. After they had all gone, there was sobbing and deep hurt on the part of the immediate family. The wife of the deceased threw herself across the casket and began to scream. It was consistent with her personality; she was that kind of person. She tended to be volatile and explosive. I expected her to handle grief in that way, and she did.

A common element in all forms of grief is the importance of tears. Never deny tears to anybody. If people want to cry in the face of tragedy, let them—in fact, encourage them. Many men need to almost pray that they will learn how to cry. On the average, women outlive men by about seven years. This is primarily because men don't know how to cry. Women handle pressure, pain, and grief much better than men do. Trying to be "a man" is not very healthy. Tears are healing. Tears are therapeutic. Tears are necessary. If there is deprivation, if someone has been wrenched from your side, give vent to your grief. Allow yourself God's gift for healing. Tears are part of that process.

The book of Job gives us some guidelines concerning the grieving process. It shows us how one man went through it. How does Job handle his grief?

I want to share with you some insights into six stages of grief that are somewhat parallel to ideas found in two contemporary books. *Good Grief* by Granger E. Westberg lists ten stages for grief.[4] It is a good book—very strong theologically. The other book is by Elizabeth Kübler-Ross and is called *On Death and Dying.*[5] She lists five stages. There is nothing sacred about the number, so I will share the six stages that I believe Job went through as he faced grief in his own life.

Numbed Shock

"Then they sat on the ground with him for seven days and seven nights. No one said a word to him, because they saw how great his suffering was" (Job 2:13). That was the best thing the three men did: They remained silent. The minute they opened their mouths they were useless. That is often true in times of grief, by the way. People come along with all kinds of inane, useless, judgmental, unfortunate, ill-timed, trite clichés. What you really need is their love, their presence, a hug, a kiss. The best thing the three men did was to sit quietly for seven days. If they had then gotten up and left, they would have ministered to Job. Unfortunately, they began to talk.

Job was going through the numbed and shocked period. When it first strikes you, you feel as though you are enveloped in cotton. You are numb. I have seen people who looked strong in the face of grief, but it was the strength of numbness. The full impact of their tragedy had not dawned on them yet.

Job goes through that now. He has lost much and is simply numb. There is nothing to say, and the friends didn't say anything.

Utter Despair

"After this, Job opened his mouth and cursed the day of his birth. He said: 'May the day of my birth perish, and the night it was said, 'A boy is born!' That day—may it turn to darkness; may God above not care about it; may not light shine upon it" (Job 3:1-4). "Why did I not perish at birth, and die as I came from the womb?" (Job 3:11). "What I feared has come upon me; what I dreaded has happened to me. I have no peace, no quietness; I have no rest, but only turmoil" (Job 3:25-26). For Job, all meaning has collapsed. Everything is foolishness. He reaches out but he feels and touches nothing. All is murky, meaningless, lonely, anxiety-ridden. Despair is everywhere.

Frances had a heart attack and a stroke. She was hospitalized for a long period of time. Her husband Ken sat with her by the day, by the hour, hour after hour. She went through therapy, and he assisted her in that process. She had another heart attack and another stroke. Again he spent days and hours. You would never see Frances without Ken at her side. Then one night I received a phone call. Ken had suddenly died. I went to the home. Frances said, "What will I do? What will I do?" She was frantic, she was lonely. "How do I pay the bills? Where will I live? What will I do? We have depended on each other. Now what?" When you have been close to somebody and he is now gone, utter despair overwhelms you when he leaves.

Excursion into Nostalgia

"One day it was so good. God was near . . . and my family was here . . . life was good, but now . . . " (see Job 29:1-6). You can feel the wrenching and the tearing in Job's words. He looks back on good memories, but now he is alone. He is broken in spirit, and his nostalgic excursion is very meaningful for him but the contrast between the then and the now hurts. When people go through the period of nostalgia, when those around you talk about the one who is deceased, encourage them. Nostalgia is helpful. Those are good memories. Those are important memories. Claim them!

Our reactions go in two directions during such times. One aspect of nostalgia is that we begin to idealize the deceased. My pastor was thirty-three when he died, and he was an excellent preacher and a fine pastor. He became even a better preacher and a better pastor after he died. Memory does that. I can think of a man who had a lovely wife for many years, and ten years ago she died. Today his memories of her are unrealistically ideal. She was magnificent, he says. Such idealization is quite common. The other aspect of nostalgia is more harmful. Often guilt sets in, and we wonder why we didn't do more. "If I had known that I was going to lose my child, we would have spent more hours together. We would have done things and we would have gone places." An old friend of mine lost a preschool child. Jim and Lana went through some dark, dark days. He wrote a paper about their personal hurt and on one page he said, "We should have spent more time together. I should have taken off time to take him to the zoo. I should have concentrated on my child. If only I could have known." The guilt of nostalgia is there: "If only I could have known that my wife was going to pass away, we would have traveled more." "If I could have known that my husband was never going to reach retirement, we would have enjoyed a lot of things and not put them off."

Anger and Resentment

Job speaks about God and says, "He throws me into the mud, and I am reduced to dust and ashes. I cry out to you, O God, but you do not answer; I stand up, but you merely look at me. You turn on me ruthlessly; with the might of your hand you attack me. You snatch me up and drive me before the wind; you toss me about in the storm. I know you will bring me down to death, to the place appointed for all the living" (Job 30:19-23). Job clenches his fist and says, "God, why did you do that?"

People in grief often become angry and resentful and feel cheated. Sometimes the anger is ventilated on their families. I have even seen it turned toward the funeral director as if he were partly responsible, or on the pastor as if he should have prayed more or somehow done something else. Often anger is directed against God. "God, you did it! Why did you do it?"

Don't be surprised when it comes. It is part of the grieving process, and it is better to admit anger than to deny it—particularly with God. God can handle all of your emotions very well.

C. S. Lewis usually wrote helpfully, with clarity and with great understanding. One of his books, though, is a "downer." It is called *A Grief Observed.*[6] In it Lewis, who married in middle age, is reflecting on his own bitterness because his wife died prematurely. Across the pages of that book you can see the words, "God, why did you do it?"

Joyce Landorf in her book *Mourning Song* talks about the two sides of our personality. One is the God-ward side, the other is the human side. The God-ward side understands: "My loved one is with you." The human side doesn't understand and gets angry. Joyce said, "After my mother died, one well-meaning Christian lady said, 'Always remember, your mother went to be with her Lord. She is probably much happier now.' " And Joyce said, "But I'm not!"[7] That is the human side. We are human and we have human needs. God can handle them. If you feel bitterness and anger, God invites you to be yourself in His presence. We are not always sure how we will handle it, but God can handle it.

A New Perspective

When your grief makes this turn, you move into a new and brighter life. "Then the Lord answered Job out of the storm. He said: 'Who is this that darkens my counsel with words without knowledge? Brace yourself like a man; I will question you, and you shall answer me. Where were you when I laid the earth's foundation? Tell me, if you understand' " (Job 38:1-4). Job is given a refresher course in theology. God reminds him that arguing about justice and injustice is an inappropriate response to the working of God, because justice and injustice is what God does or does not do. Justice is what God does. That is His standard, not our perspective. God reminds Job that He made everything, and He gives everything. He says, in effect, "What right do you have, Job, to talk about the good gifts I give you? You don't deserve any of them, and I gave them to you. They were an act of grace in the first place. I am a Giver of good gifts that you didn't deserve, and just be grateful that you ever had them at all." God gives Job a whole new perspective. He says, "What I do is right. What I do is for my glory. What I do is for your good as well." Job begins to recognize that God is on the throne and that God can handle his problems. He begins to release all the treasures he held so tightly.

Once you begin to release your treasures, God can begin to remake you. As someone has put it: "Withdraw the emotional capital from the past and reinvest it in the future." To release this loved one—it takes an average of two years, they say—is a painful, hard period of time, and sometimes you can't shorten it. But you must do it in order to gain a new perspective and then to be able to go on.

A New Beginning
"Then Job replied to the Lord: 'I know that you

can do all things; no plan of yours can be thwarted. You asked, "Who is this that obscures my counsel without knowledge?" Surely I spoke of things I did not understand, things too wonderful for me to know' " (Job 42:1-3). "God, your ways are right, and I did not understand them." Now Job is a new man with a new future. There is a future for Job because God has a future for him. There is a future for you because God has a future for you. You need not be fixated on the past. You need not stay back there. If you have gone through grief and deprivation, God can help you to reassess it and release it and then move on. He uses His people, and we will be a community of people who will stand with you in your grief. We won't say foolish things but will show you that we love you and we care. We just want to be there with you. Maybe we will sit silently and be available to you. Maybe we'll give you a strong hug or a firm handshake. You will have the assurance of our availability, our care, our prayers, our love. All of us will have days when we will need the people of God to be a healing community in our lives.

In the midst of your storm, remember this: Regardless of how high the waves, He will be there in the boat with you. You can reach out and discover that God will meet you in your grief, for He is committed to you. It may be a long period of time, but He will walk with you through the valley. Job discovered that life can become new. It can begin again.

For Further Thought

1. Do you recall your feelings when a dear friend or family member died?

2. Are you presently experiencing grief? Are you moving through it?

3. What are the typical grief stages?

4. Do you have a grieving friend who needs you? What can you do to help?

Notes

1. Edgar Jackson, *For the Living* (Des Moines: Meredith Publishing Co., 1963).
2. Lloyd H. Ahlem, *Living with Stress* (Ventura, CA: Regal Books, 1978), pp. 19-21.
3. John Claypool, *Tracks of a Fellow Struggler* (Waco, TX: Word Books, 1974), p. 86.
4. Granger E. Westberg, *Good Grief* (Philadelphia: Fortress Press, 1962).
5. Elizabeth Kübler-Ross, *On Death and Dying* (New York: Macmillan Publishing Company, Inc., 1969), pp. 38ff.
6. Joseph Bayly, *The Last Thing We Talk About* (Elgin, IL: David C. Cook Publishing Co., 1973), p. 49.
7. Joyce Landorf, *Mourning Song* (Old Tappan, NJ: Fleming H. Revell Company, 1974).

Eleven

Mid-Life Crisis

Psalm 102:1-7 is a text by a believer, a follower of Jehovah, who is lamenting all that Jerusalem is going through. It is a time of anguish over homelessness and things once had: "Hear my prayer, O Lord; let my cry for help come to you. Do not hide your face from me when I am in distress. Turn your ear to me; when I call, answer me quickly. For my days vanish like smoke; my bones burn like glowing embers. My heart is blighted and withered like grass; I forget to eat my food. Because of my loud groaning I am reduced to skin and bones. I am like a desert owl, like an owl among the ruins. I lie awake; I have become like a bird alone on a housetop."

We have all known someone who started out well. He was dedicated to Christ, active in the church, vocal about his faith. Then suddenly he dropped out. We asked the question, "Whatever happened to him? He started so well, and then something happened." Rather than continuing to enjoy life with flourish and zest, he went out in a fizzle. If you retrace his experience, you will discover that somewhere in the middle of his life he went through a crisis or a series of crises that sidetracked him.

Today we hear a lot about mid-life crisis. Technically there is no such thing as a "mid-life crisis." There are only "mid-life crises," a series of events fraught with difficulty and danger. The word *crisis* in Chinese is a character built on two other Chinese characters. The first one means "danger," the second means "opportunity." Mid-life is like that. It is susceptible to great danger, but it also promises great opportunity. You can either fall by the wayside or claim the opportunities and move ahead with even greater significance and usefulness.

Mid-life crises! Whom do they belong to? We are told that they belong to the "betweeners"—the people who have adolescent children on one side and aging parents on the other. They are the betweeners.

Women experience a two-stage crisis, we are told. The first stage is emotional, while the second is physical and has emotional ramifications. The first stage is called the "quiet nest." The children are all in school, and you breathe a great sigh of relief. You now have time on your hands, and so you scurry about, running errands. For some it is a great time for reflection. They turn inward and say, "Am I doing important things? What is my greatest value in life? Are the things I am doing really of great significance?"

The second stage is much more physical and comes somewhat later. It is called the "menopausal period" and includes significant physical changes. It is a time above all other times in life when a woman is more suspicious of her husband. It is a time when she will wonder about her worth and her value. She will need, as never before, confirmation and the evidence of love. It is a time when she goes through the hot-and-cold experiences and other physical changes. It can be a very traumatic time for a woman.

Men go through menopause too, but it is not as physical as that of women. It is more psychological and spiritual. It is a time of reevaluation: "Where am I going? I set up goals when I was a young man, and now that I am halfway through life, have I reached them? Am I where I wanted to be? What is it all about? What am I doing?" The mid-life crisis takes place between the ages of thirty and fifty. Eighty percent of the males in America—four out of five—go through a mid-life crisis of some sort or other. Twenty percent do not go through it, but, as William Hulme has written, you are not "abnormal if in midlife you discover yourself without one."[1] Don't let that become a crisis for you. Hulme continues. "I seriously doubt, however, that a person can pass through midlife in our culture without having moments of sober reflection."[2]

Mid-Life Enemies

Psalm 102 has been called "The psalm of mid-life people." When we are in mid-life we face a number of enemies.

Our bodies

"My days vanish like smoke; my bones burn like glowing embers" (v. 3). "My days are like the evening shadow; I wither away like grass" (v. 11). The body begins to wear out. Once virile and strong, now the body begins to show its weaknesses.

Jim Conway has said that the body of the mid-life person is like a building. The roof is beginning to sag. The mortar is coming out of the joints. The floors are warping, and the doors creak. The body, which was once a friend, is becoming an enemy.[3]

And its weight is rearranging itself. During Vatican II, all the presses carried a great story. It seems that when the leaders of the Roman Catholic church and the Protestant observers were gathered in Rome for the Vatican II Council, one writer, as reported by the newspaper, looked around at that gathering of religious leaders from all over the world and said, "They don't believe in girth control." What he was saying is this: "They are all getting a bit chunky." I weighed five pounds more in college than I do today, and my waist was five inches thinner then. Weight reorganizes itself as you go through mid-life.

How do we handle mid-life crises? You know how women handle them. Increasingly new bottles and jars appear on the sink. It begins to take women a half-hour or an hour to get their lives together. A little bit of this and a little bit of that, and then they emerge looking "natural." Some time later God performs a miracle and the color of their hair changes.

Men are even worse. We are a funny group. The man who has driven a four-door Ford suddenly buys a sports car, has his shirt open halfway to his stomach, and wears a gold chain with a large medallion resting on the gray hair of his chest.

Our emotions

Our text says, "My heart is blighted and withered like grass. I forget to eat my food." In the midst of your emotional stress and strain, you have a time of evaluation and of asking important questions: "What am I doing? What is my purpose in life? Am I contributing anything worthwhile?" It is a time of great stress, and your appetite is sometimes gone. Sometimes you cannot sleep very well. "I lie awake; I have become like a bird alone on a housetop" (Ps. 102:7). While your college-age student sleeps like a log through the night, you and your mid-life mate pass each other in the living room at three in the morning. Sleep fails you at times. There is so much on your mind. Mid-life stress is fraught with emotional pressure.

How do people handle it? Sometimes they go through deep depression. They "feel trapped like a rabbit," says Jim Conway. You have one of two choices: "You can either wait for the hunter, or you can chew off your leg and escape and go through life maimed."⁴ That is a bit pessimistic, but what he is saying is that mid-life can be a time of great stress that leaves people scarred unless it is dealt with.

Our work

We feel as though we were on a treadmill. "All day long my enemies taunt me; those who rail against me use my name as a curse" (Ps. 102:8). This is a picture of people in our workaday world. You find that you are in competition with others. They are vying for your post and waiting for you to fall because they want to take your place. Nobody

really wants to support you. They are all compet-
ing with you. Lyndon Johnson was awakened
every morning by his dad who said, "Get up, Lyndon, or every boy in the neighborhood will have a
head start on you."[5] Compete! Get going! Be off
and running! Work! Work! Work!

Some people feel pressure like that, and they
cannot handle it. They want to drop out. I think of
a man who pastored a large church in the Mid-
west, and in his middle years he couldn't quite
handle the pressure any more. He couldn't meet
exacting demands of his work day after day. He
finally took off, and for nine months he traveled
around the United States on a motorcycle.

At the age of forty-five a friend of mine, after
having had years of practice as an M.D., sold
everything he owned and went back to school. He
learned another specialty. Today he is a very gifted
obstetrician and gynecologist in a different loca-
tion. He found that the only way he could handle
mid-life stress was to say, "I am not happy with life
as it is." So he made a change in direction.

People often do that. For example, more and
more people in mid-life are entering seminary
these days. They have had other careers, and now
they feel called by God to serve Him. A variety of
things happen as people deal with the anxiety of
their work.

Our family

It may sound strange, but one's family can be
an enemy for the mid-life person. "Let this be written for a future generation, that a people not yet
created may praise the Lord" (Ps. 102:18).

Psychologist Keith Edwards has said that one of the things that people want to do is to pass on to their children and grandchildren things of value and worth.[6] If they don't feel they are doing that, they go through great depression. "What am I passing on to my progeny—my children, my grandchildren?" they ask. Some men have said, "If it weren't for my family, I would not work as I do. I am under stress and pressure because I have to do this. We'll lose our home and all that we own. Unless I work every day, I fail my family."

We accumulate things, don't we? When Nancy and I were married on August 9, 1958, we piled everything we owned in all the world into a Chevy and traveled two thousand miles from the church to California to go to school. Three years later we traveled from California to Boston and drove thirty-one hundred miles and pulled all of our earthly possessions in a five-by-eight U-Haul. Eleven years ago we moved to California—in the front end of an Allied van. Recently we moved to San Diego—and took up about half of the van. I don't know where we got all this stuff. Some of it is early Salvation Army, and some is who knows what. But I feel that somehow I have to provide this for my family. Somehow my family needs me, they need what I can provide, they need the things I can give them. People in mid-life sometimes can't stand such pressures, and so they look for a way out. That is why we see people who have been married for twenty-five or thirty years going out and getting a divorce. We say, "Oh, how tragic!" Or the husband may go out and have an affair to discover something about his lost youth and his vitality. We say, "What a terrible way to handle a crisis!"

God

"For I eat ashes as my food and mingle my drink with tears because of your great wrath, for you have taken me up and thrown me aside" (vv. 9-10). "In the course of my life he broke my strength; he cut short my days" (v. 23). Sometimes mid-life people say, "God did it. Why did He allow that? Why did He send that?" Jim Conway says, "The mid-life man pictures God leaning over the banister of heaven, grinning fiendishly and pointing a long, bony finger as he says, 'You despicable, disgraceful Christian! . . . selfish . . . filled with lust . . . lazy . . . disgusting . . . .' He says to God, 'You made me this way . . . you are the one who is really, ultimately to blame for the mess I'm in now!'"[7] Many feel that God is bringing pressure on their lives, and so they just back off. All of a sudden they no longer are part of a church council or committee, or they stop attending Sunday School, and they stop going to worship services. They no longer pray before meals; they are far away from God. You shake your head and you say, "How tragic!" The enemy has conquered.

Mid-Life Allies

But I don't want to leave you there. Second Timothy contains a healthy biblical response to mid-life crises. Paul is writing to Timothy who had trusted Christ fifteen years prior to this occasion. For fifteen years Timothy had served God, and Paul looked on him as his younger brother in the faith. Timothy had been triumphant, strong and vital, but now you receive the impression he is getting timid and weak. So in 2 Timothy 1:7 Paul says, "God did not give us a spirit of timidity." He says in chapter 2, "Be strong." He tells Timothy to get into the Word and become a servant who can interpret it correctly. He says, "Do the work of an evangelist." All through the book we find these words of encouragement. "Come on, Timothy, get on with it!" Louis Palau has said that 2 Timothy was probably written to a man in mid-life crisis. It mentions a number of allies for mid-life people.

The power of memory

"I thank God, whom I serve, as my forefathers did, with a clear conscience, as night and day I constantly remember you in my prayers. Recalling your tears, I long to see you, so that I may be filled with joy. I have been reminded of your sincere faith, which first lived in your grandmother Lois and in your mother Eunice and, I am persuaded, now lives in you also" (2 Tim. 1:3-5).

That is my inheritance as well. Personally, I am grateful to my mom for her faith and her love and her teaching, and I trust you are grateful for yours also. We are so blessed! Paul says, "Think back on your past. It serves you well. You walked with God and met Him through people who touched your life." It may have been grandparents; it may have been parents; it may have been friends—but let God jog your memory and remind you of your past. You may be afar off today, but you could again be where you once were.

The power of fresh commitment

"For this reason I remind you to fan into flame the gift of God" (2 Tim. 1:6). Every Christian has a gift, and Paul is saying, "Fan the flickering flame and let it surge up into a great and strong flame."

Make a fresh commitment. Don't settle for where you are—make a fresh commitment to Him. Allow God to do a new work in you, regardless of where you are today. If you are going through some of the things I have talked about and you have bottomed out a bit, you don't need to stay there. You can rise again and find forgiveness and cleansing and restoration and healing. God will do a new work in you. Fan afresh the flame of your faith and of your gifts.

The power of counsel

"So do not be ashamed to testify about our Lord, or ashamed of me his prisoner. But join with me in suffering for the gospel, by the power of God" (v. 8). Paul counsels Timothy further in verse 12: "That is why I am suffering as I am. Yet I am not ashamed, because I know whom I have believed, and am convinced that he is able to guard what I have entrusted to him for that day." All through the book Paul counsels Timothy by word, by life, by admonition, by model. One of the great resources that God has given us are Christian counselors—men and women trained and equipped to understand our feelings, our depression, our discouragement. We can turn to them for strength as they enable us to see ourselves as we are and to claim health and healing again. Don't be afraid to use the great resources that God has placed at the disposal of the Christian in our day. There are many Christians across our land to whom God has given great gifts to minister to us. It may be a mate, or a Sunday School teacher, or a pastor, or a friend. We need them!

One thing we all need in mid-life is more exercise. Sometimes in the middle of life we get so busy that we don't take time to keep our bodies healthy. My mother went bowling with my daughter recently, and she bowled four games. That is one of the reasons why my eighty-one-year-old mother is still healthy to serve God. She can still minister to people because she has worked at keeping physically healthy. She was much more sickly in her younger years. Then she lost weight and did a number of things to stay healthy. Get your exercise; eat properly; have plenty of rest; find ways to become absorbed in healthy things once again. Use your life and your energies. Find fresh ways to serve Him again. Read helpful books by people like Jim Conway and Sally Conway.[8] One is from a man's perspective, the other from a woman's perspective.

The power of the Scriptures
"Do your best to present yourself to God as one approved, a workman who does not need to be ashamed and who correctly handles the word of truth" (2 Tim. 2:15). It is "useful for teaching, rebuking, correcting and training in righteousness, so that the man of God may be thoroughly equipped for every good work" (2 Tim. 3:16-17). Without being overly simplistic, I want to say that people who are going their own way, away from God, are not people who are in the Word of God. But people who are growing in Christian maturity, who are alive spiritually, are people in the Word. If that sounds simple, it is nevertheless true. God has given us a source of strength and power in His Word.

Jerry and Mary White write that the pelicans of

Monterey, California were spoiled birds. They would watch the fishermen come in from their day of fishing. As the fishermen would clean the fish, they would throw all the leavings to the pelicans. The birds just sat around and ate well. Day after day the fishermen came, and day after day the pelicans sat around and ate. They became fat and sassy and lazy. The best-fed pelicans in all the world were the ones in Monterey.

Then the fishermen decided to take the fish scraps and use them for commercial purposes. Very quickly the pelicans became thin and gaunt, and some of them died. They had forgotten how to fish. So some of their cousins from Southern California who knew how to fish were brought up to Monterey, and they began to fish there. Those lazy cousins of theirs in Monterey watched what they were doing, and learned how to fish again, and soon the famine was over.[9]

A lot of Christians are like the pelicans of Monterey. They come to church and we feed them, but they really have never learned to fish for themselves. They get thin and gaunt. So they need the encouragement that Paul gave to Timothy: "Study to show yourself." The text doesn't say, "Ask your pastor to study to show himself approved unto God." The text is for you—for each of us—and it tells us to read for ourselves, to be personal gleaners of the Bible's truth and resources so that we will continue to grow.

The power of restoration

"Get Mark and bring him with you, because he is helpful to me in my ministry" (2 Tim. 4:11). At the end of Paul's first missionary journey, he sat down with Barnabas and said, "Let's plan journey number two." And they said as they chatted together, "Who should we bring?" Barnabas said, "Of course we will bring Mark." And Paul said, "Of course we will not bring Mark." So they had a friendly discussion, and each went his own way. Paul acquired a new associate named Silas, and Barnabas went off with Mark. Barnabas poured his life into Mark—and now, as Paul is in the last winter of his life, he says, "Bring my good friend Mark. He is helpful for the ministry." That is the power of restoration.

Nobody needs to settle for final failure. You can be restored in your spiritual life whether you are in mid-life, or early life, or later life. If you are away from God, you need not stay there. Mark was restored, and you can be restored and live life to the full in the blessing of God through Jesus Christ. That is the gospel! That is the good news! He is a God who forgives, who heals, who restores, who uses again.

Ray and Anne Ortlund wrote a book called *The Best Half of Life*.[10] It refers to the last half. You can look back on your life and say, "Oh, all that I used to have—all the plans I had—here I am, and I have not achieved them." You can turn sour and give up on life. Or you can say, "I have learned some lessons along the way, and I have more to offer, more to do; I understand better as I reach the second half of life." Ortlund is right; it is the best half! I look back on my younger years and I say, "Oh, those were good years!" But I would not go back there for the life of me. The second half is better! Take it and claim all the lessons you have learned and all the grace you have experienced. Be able to

say as did Jim Conway at the end of his book,
"Humpty Dumpty is together again. And it is not
the same Humpty. I am a new man—more mature,
more understanding, more sensitive. I can serve
God again."

It all depends on you. He is the God who makes
people new.

For Further Thought

1. How would you define a mid-life crisis?

2. Are you in the midst of such a crisis?

3. What are you doing to cope with it?

4. What are the allies that could assist you?

5. Have you offered yourself as a friend to a mid-
   life sufferer? Your friendship could be cru-
   cial.

Notes

   1. William Hulme, *Mid-Life Crises* (Philadelphia: Westminster
Press, 1980), p. 21.
   2. Ibid., p. 21.
   3. Jim Conway, *Men in Mid-Life Crisis* (Elgin, IL: David C. Cook
Publishing Co., 1978), p. 83.
   4. Ibid., p. 22.
   5. Hulme, *Mid-Life Crises*, p. 25.
   6. Personal note to author, March 22, 1981.
   7. Conway, *Men in Mid-Life*, p. 67.
   8. Jim Conway and Sally Conway, *You and Your Husband in Mid-
Life Crisis* (Elgin, IL: David C. Cook Publishing Co., 1980).
   9. Jerry and Mary White, *The Christian in Mid-Life* (Colorado
Springs: Navpress, 1980), pp. 129-130.
   10. Ray and Anne Ortlund, *The Best Half of Life* (Waco: Word Books,
1976).

Twelve

Money

"But godliness with contentment is great gain. For we brought nothing into the world, and we can take nothing out of it. But if we have food and clothing, we will be content with that. People who want to get rich fall into temptation and a trap and into many foolish and harmful desires that plunge men into ruin and destruction. For the love of money is a root of all kinds of evil. Some people, eager for money, have wandered from the faith and pierced themselves with many griefs" (1 Tim. 6:6-10).

Money can either be an appreciated friend or a destructive enemy. It has been estimated that 70 percent of the worries of modern America are money-oriented.[1] Money is a cause for worry for many people.

Or consider a study that was done by the U.S. Bureau of Labor Statistics. A survey of 10,813 families in ninety-one American cities concluded that the average American family spent each year

$400 more than it earned.[2] No wonder the Bible says so much about money! God knew we would have trouble with it. One-third of Jesus' parables are about money. Every sixth verse in Matthew, Mark, and Luke is about money and resources.

But money is neutral. Money in itself is not sinful. To be rich is not to be carnal. To be poor is not to be spiritual. Some of the godly people of the Old Testament were wealthy: Abraham, Job, David, Solomon. Each had glorious moments spiritually, and yet they were rich people. Wealth is not in itself sinful. It has power, and power is either destructive or good. Everything depends on what you do with wealth—how you handle it, how you receive it.

Let's look first at money's power for evil.

Covetousness—The Snare

Covetousness is a snare (1 Tim. 6). Covetousness is the inordinate desire to have more than you possess. It is the drive to get more of everything because you are never satisfied. The verse before us is often misquoted. Some people tell us that money is the root of all evil. But the Bible doesn't say that. It says that "the love of money is a root of all kinds of evil." It is a root of all other kinds of sin: lying (1 Kings 22); theft (Josh. 7); domestic problems (Prov. 15:27); murder (Ezek. 22). Covetousness often gives birth to other sins.

But covetousness is built on illusions. "People who want to get rich fall into temptation and a trap" (1 Tim. 6:9). A trap is something that snares us. It makes us prisoners.

An animal is often trapped by placing food in a snare. The animal is enticed by the food and is then ensnared by the trap. We had mice for a while, and so we bought traps. We put cheese on them, and a mouse came and took the cheese, and that was the end of the mouse! To the mouse it looked good, but it led to his destruction.

Covetousness is built on illusions

Covetousness seems to offer good things. It is attractive and you say, "Oh, that looks good." But when you fall into its trap, it is to your own destruction.

One of its illusions is that *wealth brings happiness.* But nothing woven into the fabric of wealth guarantees that it will make you happy. On the contrary, a lot of people who have wealth are very unhappy. For example, Solomon had an annual income of about twenty million dollars. He had a home that took thirteen years to build. He had a throne made of ivory and gold. He had forty thousand stalls for his horses. And he had— incredibly—seven hundred wives and three hundred concubines. We are told that his table was a nonstop banquet including sheep, oxen and fowl. He had a large family, enormous resources, and a huge income.[3]

What did all of this lead to? Read about it in Ecclesiastes: "Vanity of vanities; all is vanity" (Eccles. 1:2, *KJV*). Solomon says to us, "Everything is meaningless." Was he happy? Not really. The illusion that Satan gives to us is this: "For me things will be different. For Solomon something went wrong. If I had what he had, I would be happy." Perhaps you once wished to have what other people had. You said, "Oh, if I only had that!" But then you learned about the great unhappiness in their lives. Wealth really didn't offer what they thought it would. It was a trap.

The other illusion is that *wealth brings security*. But rather than bringing security, it often creates insecurity. Wealthy people often live in fear of the next issue of the *Wall Street Journal*. They never know what is going to happen to the stock market. It goes up and down. They don't know what is going to happen in industry, they don't know what is going to happen to the money situation, they don't know when mortgage rates will go up or when their cash flow will go down. Sometimes the more you have the more insecure you become.

A New Testament parable tells us about a man who had huge crops. He said, "I know what I'll do. I'll tear down my barns and build bigger ones. It's about time to relax and take it easy. I'll eat, drink and be merry." Then the Lord comes to him and says, "You are a fool. Tonight it will be all over. You brought nothing into the world, and you are going to take nothing out of the world." The biblical truth of the matter is that happiness is found in Christ and in people, not in things. The happiest people in the world are those who have friends and who have the Lord.

Recently eighteen people dropped in on us almost by surprise. After they left, Nancy and I said, "We are really rich!" All of them were Christian friends. There is nothing richer than the Body of Christ. When you are low or high, when you are dejected or encouraged, to be able to rejoice with others who can rejoice with you and to be able to weep with those with whom you can weep, you are rich indeed.

And if you are in Christ, that is happiness indeed. Nothing else, no one else, can provide that kind of security. The only security that is guaranteed 100 percent is what Christ gives you. Nothing is better or safer than that. His presence in your life, His faithfulness to you—these are absolutely guaranteed. He will not be fickle. He will always be there. Security is found in Him, not in things.

Covetousness results in destruction

But covetousness is not only built on illusions. It often results in destruction as well. "People who want to get rich fall into temptation and a trap and into many foolish and harmful desires that plunge men into ruin and destruction" (1 Tim. 6:9). The Greek word for "plunge" here means literally "drown." Those insatiable, inordinate drives can push you under. They can destroy you.

What gets destroyed? For one thing, faith. Money, as the Roman proverb puts it, is like sea water. The more you drink, the more you want. You never get to the place where you say, "Enough!" Suddenly your faith falters and is soon sacrificed on the altar of wealth. Once it was King Jesus on the throne of your life. But now He is pushed aside, and there is a new king—the almighty dollar. When faith is sacrificed as you pursue more and more wealth, you have made a bad bargain.

What gets destroyed? For another thing, your family. When you wander from the faith, you pierce yourself "with many griefs" (1 Tim. 6:10). You may find that as you pursue wealth—and perhaps achieve it—you leave your family behind. Thousands of people in this city have lusted after things and have lost their families. At the end of your life when you see, gathered around your bed, the faces of a family that loves you and loves God, you know there is nothing to compare with that. It is priceless. It is worth much more than the world's largest bank account.

Johnny Carson is a symbol of what can happen. He makes over a million dollars a year, but his third wife recently divorced him. His name is a household word, he is famous, he has enormous talents and resources. But each of his three marriages has been shattered in the midst of all that. A bad bargain!

The flip side of our study is much more positive. Contentment is a possibility for the believer. Contentment is the biblical standard. But contentment is not complacency, it is not laziness, it is not surrender. It comes in the midst of the battle, in the middle of your quest to be successful. Contentment means to discover rest and peace and balance in Christ.

Contentment is a matter of attitude

"I know what it is to be in need, and I know what it is to have plenty. I have learned the secret of being content in any and every situation, whether well fed or hungry, whether living in plenty or in want" (Phil. 4:12). Good days or bad days, much or nothing, well fed or hungry, great resources or none at all—Paul could say, "In both I have discovered contentment." To know that your life does not consist of the things you have, to be secure and at rest and at peace with what you have—that is the attitude of a believing heart.

Contentment is a lesson to learn

"I am not saying this because I am in need, for I have learned to be content whatever the circumstances" (Phil. 4:11). The Greek tense of "learned" is *punctiliar*. It is a point in time, and it means this: There was a point in time when Paul made a turn in his life. He came to that place in his life where a lesson was learned, and from that time on he was a man who lived according to that lesson. We assume that he didn't go to a money management seminar. At some point in Paul's life the Holy Spirit, working through circumstances, enabled him to come to the place where he could say, "I am now content."

How can we learn the same lesson? George Bowman has written a helpful book called *How to Succeed with Your Money*. He talks about the ten/seventy/twenty plan.[4] I commend it to you. Give the first 10 percent to God. Live off the next 70 percent. It pays for all your living expenses—house, insurance, everything. Twenty percent is then left for discretionary purposes: for investment, for savings, for response to special opportunities to serve God. People who have put this plan into practice are always available when special opportunities arise. Someone may come up to you and say, "You know, there is a special opportunity to serve God." And you may have to say, "Well, I am going to have to wait awhile. I don't have anything now." Most of us have never learned to have discretionary funds for opportunities.

I once knew a man who cast everything in monetary terms. Whenever there was a problem, in his mind it was always financial. Whether the church was in a building program, or giving to missions, or whatever, he would always complain about our spending too much money. One day several years ago he came and sat down in my office and began to cry. He said, "I have been hard on you. The reason is, that I have lived on 105 percent of my income, and every time an opportunity came to serve God I felt so guilty that I made you carry my guilt."

If you live beyond your means, you will always feel that other people are wrong in their investments and commitments. Opportunities come to serve God, and the only way you can handle them is to complain. But when you begin to budget your resources, and don't spend 105 percent of what you have, you will be able to respond to opportunities when they come—no matter how much or how little you have. I have known people who depend on fixed income and Social Security but who always have discretionary money left over because they have chosen to live on 70 percent of their resources. It doesn't matter how much you have; it is how well you plan.

I commend the ten/seventy/twenty plan to you. Eliot Janeway says you always ought to have six months of income set aside. How many of you have six months of income available? Six days? Six hours? Often we are pressed because we spend everything we have.

Serve God with your income. Live on just a portion of it. Set some of it aside to be able to make investments, to be able to care for debts, to be able to help people in need, to be able to serve God.

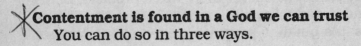
Contentment is found in a God we can trust
You can do so in three ways.

First, you can trust His providence: "I rejoice greatly in the Lord that at last you have renewed your concern for me. Indeed, you have been concerned but you had no opportunity to show it" (Phil. 4:10). "Providence" comes from *pro* ("before") and *video* ("to see"). Providence means "seeing before." God sees your whole life. He sees it before you even get there, and in every situation of life He can give you whatever you need. He lavishes His providential care on you, and you can trust Him for it. He cares for you. He is committed to you. He puts His arms of care about you and says, "I see beforehand. I know what you are going to go through, and I can meet you there. You can trust me for that." Paul did, because God worked in the lives of the Philippians. God will work in your life as well.

Second, you can trust His power: "I can do everything through him who gives me strength" (Phil. 4:13). God says, "I will enable you. I will give you my power. When you go through difficulty, trial and testing, my availability and my strength can meet you there." Through trials, through difficult times, Paul had been initiated into God's power to care.

Warren Wiersbe, one of my favorite writers and preachers, says that he was once flying over New York. The plane was going to be late. The pilot announced over the intercom that they would be at least an hour late. As they circled around in their flight pattern over New York, one of the passengers expressed the world's approach to problems. He said, "Bring out the booze."[5]

The world gets very uptight with problems. Paul doesn't say, "Bring out the booze." He says,

"My God is able." Whatever your problem, God is able to provide His strength and meet you. "I can do everything through Him who enables and strengthens me." That is His power to care.

Third, you can trust His promise: "And my God will meet all your needs according to his glorious riches in Christ Jesus" (Phil. 4:19). Out of His great resources, you give and you do and you serve and you work. And He says, "Out of my great resources in Christ Jesus I will meet your needs." You are not called to be lazy. You are called to be a good steward. You are called to be a faithful worker. You are called to use industry and initiative. Then trust His power and His promise to meet your needs. "Be anxious for nothing." "Trust me," says the Lord.

Recently I went to a local shop in the little community where we live. It has a shoe store and lock shop in the same small building. I waited in line. Finally it was my turn. I took off my shoe and showed it to the gentleman. I said, "This is a shoe I have really learned to love. It has been resoled three times, and now it has another hole in the sole on both sides. Look at this crack between the sole and the body of the shoe. Also, it's all scuffed here. Look at this shoe. Do you think it's worth fixing once more?" He said, "I don't know. I'm the locksmith."

Have you noticed how often people go to the wrong sources for their answers? We go to money and we say, "I want security." And money says, "I don't know." Then the Lord says, "Come to me. Trust me. Serve me. I will meet your needs. I am worthy." "My God shall supply all your needs in Christ Jesus."

For Further Thought

1. How are you doing with your money management?

2. How do you handle covetousness in your life?

3. Are you moving towards contentment?

4. Where does Jesus Christ fit into your financial picture?

Notes

1. George W. Bowman, *How to Succeed with Your Money* (Chicago: Moody Press, 1974), p. 46.
2. Ibid., p. 47.
3. Leslie B. Flynn, *Your God and Your Gold* (Williamsport, PA: Heatherstone Publications, Inc., 1961), p. 112.
4. Bowman, *How to Succeed*, pp. 157-167.
5. Warren Wiersbe, *Be Joyful* (Wheaton, IL: Victor Books, 1974), p. 124.

Thirteen

Ethics

"Therefore, as God's chosen people, holy and dearly loved, clothe yourselves with compassion, kindness, humility, gentleness and patience. Bear with each other and forgive whatever grievances you may have against one another. Forgive as the Lord forgave you. And over all these virtues put on love, which binds them all together in perfect unity. Let the peace of Christ rule in your hearts, since as members of one body you were called to peace. And be thankful. Let the word of Christ dwell in your richly as you teach and admonish one another with all wisdom, and as you sing psalms, hymns and spiritual songs with gratitude in your hearts to God. And whatever you do, whether in word or deed, do it all in the name of the Lord Jesus, giving thanks to God the Father through him" (Col. 3:12-17).

We live in a tangled, complex world—a world that heaves under the pressures of political intrigue, that experiences the dual problems of poverty and affluence, that is threatened within by racial conflict, that asks questions about nuclear disarmament or the acceleration of arms. It's a world that is threatened by all sorts of theories concerning morality and by descending levels of morality in our society. Problems exist between labor and management. Problems exist between parents and children, between husbands and wives. And we are thrust into the middle of this complex maze in our tangled world, and we say, "Be a Christian there." Perhaps never in the history of the Christian Church has the Christian faced more complexity in his decision making than today. It calls for maturity, the kind of maturity that says, "My faith means something in our kind of world." God calls us to be His people in a world that knows Him not.

Ethical Possibilities

Ethics relates to decision making. What does it mean to do the will of God personally and socially? There are three options, three ethical possibilities, in our world.

The existential option

If it feels good, do it. The high priest of this movement is Hugh Hefner, the editor/publisher of *Playboy* Magazine. He grew up in a fundamentalist Bible church in Chicago, rejected fundamentalism, and today is an articulate spokesman for the existential option so contrary to biblical standards. Hugh Hefner is a man whose philosophy has infiltrated our whole culture. His thesis can be summed up in three words: freedom, enjoyment, responsibility. Hefner says in essence: "You should not be restricted by laws. Don't let religious laws restrain you. Do what you want to do in freedom. Enjoy your life. Don't allow the shackles of any restrictive system to bind you. Enjoy yourself. If you don't harm anybody, do whatever you wish and enjoy it. Have the freedom to do it and the freedom to enjoy it. Just so you don't hurt anybody." You can see where that takes you. In morality: If it doesn't hurt anybody, do it. You don't have to be married. In business: If you get ahead and you don't hurt anybody, do it, even if you cheat in certain areas. Freedom, enjoyment, responsibility—many march to that drumbeat in our day.

The situational option

The second ethical option sounds a little better and is often attractive to the believing community. It is called situation ethics. If it is loving, do it. The high priest of this movement is Joseph Fletcher, a theologian who teaches at the Episcopal Seminary in Cambridge, Massachusetts. Like that of Hugh Hefner, Joseph Fletcher's thesis is an anti-law approach as well. He says that all the "thou shalt nots" are absorbed in one "thou shalt love." That sounds good to people, and they are taken in by it. They say, "Now that seems to be very biblical. If it's loving, do it."

But listen to one of Fletcher's illustrations.[1] A woman is in a prison camp during the war. She has a husband and children back home. The only way she can be released from prison is to become pregnant. Fletcher says that the Christian thing for her to do is to get a soldier to have intercourse with her so that she then becomes pregnant and can go home and do the loving thing and be with her children and her husband. Forget "Thou shalt not commit adultery." Do the loving thing for your family. Love dictates everything, setting aside the biblical commandments. Do the loving thing.

Certain problems immediately arise. For one thing, we are spring-loaded in the direction of self-ishness, not love. If you throw us into the air, we don't come down loving. Throw us into the air, and we come down with self-interest. If we were all completely sanctified, then you could tell us to do the loving thing. But we are not. What we do we may call love, but it may be very selfish indeed.

The second part of the problem with situation ethics is that it talks about love for man but forgets about love for God. How do you love God? By doing His will, obeying His Word, keeping His commandments. If love is only related to others and not to God Himself, then it is a muffled and distorted form of love.

The biblical option

The third ethical possibility is the biblical option: If it is Christian, do it. You pull together all the facts, and then you bring the Word of God to bear upon them. At the intersection of life and His Word, we make our decisions with the full facts and the full impact of Scripture. That is where decision making that is Christian exists. It is challenging and demanding and difficult, but that is what God calls us to.

Ethical Principles

Our text deals with the ethical principles of biblical decision making.

The wholeness of life

You cannot just take a part of life and say that it alone is sacred. "And whatever you do, whether in word or deed, do it all in the name of the Lord Jesus, giving thanks to God the Father through him" (Col. 3:17). Every experience in life is sacred—or ought to be. You cannot say, "This is my secular life, and that is my sacred life." You cannot say, "My dating and recreation are secular, while my church attendance, worship, care group, and Bible study are sacred. They are two separate worlds." For the Christian there is only one world, and the umbrella of faith has to extend over the whole package. You must say, "Every area of my life is now sacred." What you do on a date is sacred. What you do when you close a deal is sacred. What you do when you fill out your expense account is sacred. What you do when you talk to your neighbor is sacred. How you treat the man at the service station is sacred. "Whatever you do . . . in word or deed" is sacred. So you don't say, "Now it's time for secular activities." There is no time out. All time is sacred.

Dr. Bob Cook, for many years the president of Youth for Christ and in more recent years the president of King's College, is a man who has articulated biblical ethics in an extraordinary fashion throughout his life. I have shared vacations, business, and worship experiences with him, and for him all of life is sacred. His principle is this: "Do anything you want to if in the middle of it you can pray and ask God's blessing upon it." Try that on for size! Young person, in the middle of your date can you at that moment say, "Lord, bless this"? Can you go anywhere this week and feel

that it is impossible to ask God to bless it? Then
you have decided that the activity is not Christian.
All of life is sacred—in business, at home, playing
ball, dating, or whatever. All is sacred. In the
midst of whatever you're doing, can you ask God to
bless it?

The complexity of decision making

We don't want to suggest for a minute that
decision making is easy. Many areas of decision
making have become very difficult. "God's chosen
people, holy and dearly loved, clothe yourselves
with compassion, kindness, humility, gentleness
and patience" (Col. 3:12-13). Such things are
never easy to do. "Bear with each other." That is
tough. "Forgive whatever grievances you may have
against one another." That is often extremely difficult.

Decision making isn't easy. It is sometimes difficult to do and difficult to stick with. Sometimes
you want to say "No!" and the Bible says, "Bear
with it." You want to strike back, but the Word of
God says, "Bear with one another." Be suspicious
if all of life becomes simple in terms of decision
making. Because life is complex, our decisions will
often be complex.

Two Israelite spies stopped in and stayed with a
lady named Rahab. She hid them. There was a
knock on the door. She opened the door. Those
outside said, "Do you have two Israelite spies
here?"

What was Rahab supposed to say? She hid
them and covered up for them.

Now the Bible is not suggesting that you are to
be a liar. What the Bible is suggesting is that

sometimes there are two choices, and neither one of them is particularly good. You choose the lesser of the two evils, and that becomes the ethical good, because at times you must choose even when neither choice is good.

What do you do when you go to vote in an election, and you look at the two names on the ballot, and you say, "I should have stayed home!" The Christian does not leave the ballot place and say, "I can't vote." You say, "I don't like either of these choices. Neither one expresses to my mind the biggest and the best for our city or nation. But I will make the choice that to me is the better of the two." Tragic moral choices make decision making difficult. You vote because you must vote. Then you support the one who is elected. Christians must do so even though they don't like either choice. Some things are difficult to live with. Even after you have made the decision you are not particularly happy with it, and people may not be happy with you.

I have been almost a complete supporter of the Moral Majority, but not quite. I do not accept their platform on prayer in public schools. I don't want my children to participate in prayer led by Mormons and Jehovah's Witnesses and unbelievers and liberals and people who deny the faith. Why should they be leading my children in prayer? I stand with the other things the Moral Majority stands for. But we should teach our children how to pray at home, and we should teach them how to pray in church. We don't need people who don't love Jesus leading them in prayer in school. But when I say that, I may sound like a liberal to some people. The fact of the matter is, however, that you must make decisions that you think are spiritually mature, that are for the best for all concerned. Your decisions may not always have the blessing of everyone, but you must make them even if they are controversial. Take a stand for what you believe is right biblically in terms of your Christian faith even though it is difficult to do and painful to live with.

The primacy of love

"And over all these virtues put on love, which binds them all together in perfect unity" (Col. 3:14). The primacy of love that we are talking about here is not that of situation ethics. It is the love that expresses itself in love for God and love for neighbor. "Love the Lord your God with all your heart and with all your soul and with all your strength . . . and, . . . your neighbor as yourself" (Luke 10:27). It is the two-foci approach of loving God with all our hearts and loving our neighbor as ourselves. Jesus says, "Go out into the world and have that kind of love." Martin Luther used to say, "Love God and do as you please." I would add, "Love God and your neighbor and do as you please." If you really loved our Lord and you loved people, and if you followed what that love led you to do, you would be moving in a healthy direction spiritually.

The imitation of Christ

"Bear with each other and forgive whatever grievances you may have against one another" (Col. 3:13). Forgive as the Lord forgave you. That is Christlikeness. Those of us who take seriously what it means to be born again, to be redeemed,

Paul calls us to Christlikeness. Let Christ be in you. Have the mind of Christ. Hebrews 12 talks about being a follower of Jesus.

Charles Sheldon wrote a book years ago called *In His Steps.*² Blow the dust off your copy of that book. It has some good ideas. Suppose you are in a difficult situation in business and you are about to close a deal. You wonder, "What shall I say? How shall I do this?" Ask the question, "What would Jesus Christ do?" If you are wondering about dating a young lady, ask this: "What would Christ have me do?" You are filling out your 1040 form. What could Christ co-sign? Forgive as He forgave. Let His mind be in you. Be like Him.

Ethical Procedure

Let's review the procedural steps of biblical ethics. How would you deal with a specific problem?

First: what are the facts?

When you are going to vote, you ought to sit down with all the facts before you and read them carefully. Read both sides, not just what your neighbor recommends. Look the facts over, and then draw the curtain and make a decision based on carefully considered information. Don't do anything before you know the facts.

One of the liabilities in the life of the Apostle Peter was that he often made a decision and then found out the facts afterwards. He always got himself into trouble with that approach. And Peter has more relatives in the Church than we know what to do with. I have been Peter-like on occasion, haven't you? You have gone ahead and said, "This is what we need to do." Then you find out that what you have done was wrong because it wasn't based on all the facts you knew. You then apologize, you stumble a bit, and you do it again. Psychologists talk about suspending closure. Don't tie a decision up until you know the facts.

Second: what does the Bible say?

What does the Word of God say? Get the facts and then compare them with the Word of God. Take some paper and write down all of the information—the pros, the cons, the strengths, the weaknesses. Then take out your Bible and go through everything step by step. What does my Bible say? What about its commandments? Many people today are allergic to commandments, but the biblical laws have not been changed. Exodus 20 is still in your Bible. Deuteronomy 5 is still there. It is still God's standard. "Remember the Sabbath day to keep it holy." The Sabbath day changed to Sunday, but how do you keep Sunday holy? Think that one through. "Honor your father and mother." How are you doing on that one? "Thou shalt not commit adultery." One man with one woman, husband and wife for life, no options, no multiple choices—how are you doing on that? "Thou shalt not steal." That law has not changed. Do you have any idea how much money it costs industry and retail marketing each year because of theft on the part of its employees? That is why they put guards at the exits where the employees punch out. It is because millions of dollars are being stolen each year by employees who want to take the products home and think they deserve them. "Thou shalt not steal."

If there isn't a specific command, look for the

164 Clearing Life's Hurdles

principle involved. When you are speeding, is there a biblical principle about driving your car too fast? The Bible doesn't mention freeways, but talks about obeying laws. The powers that be are ordained of God, and those laws exist for your good (see Rom. 13:1-5). When a Christian follows biblical standards but drives recklessly, he is being inconsistent. How about overeating? "Your body is a temple of the Holy Spirit" (1 Cor. 6:19). Biblical principles cover many areas of our lives.

Third: what is its impact?

Therefore, if what I eat causes my brother to fall into sin, I will never eat meat again, so that I will not cause him to fall" (1 Cor. 8:13). We are not islands. We are peninsulas, connected to the Body of Christ. What you do affects others. We should affect people positively, in godly ways. Even though what you do may be right for you, it may be harmful for someone you influence, therefore, the answer is don't do it. How does what you do affect your children, your parents, your employees, your neighbors?

Fourth: how will you test it?

You can test a problem by bringing it to the light (Eph. 5:11). Bring your difficult decisions to a Bible study group that is praying for you and say, "Here is my decision. What do you think?" Perhaps they will look it over and say, "That looks good to us. Let's pray about it and do it." Or they may say, "No, you shouldn't do that." You then say, "Thanks for your leadership and your guidance. I won't do it." This is the test of bringing it to the light of godly people.

Fifth: now what do we do?

Once you have gone through the process, responsibility says that you must do something. It is irresponsible to think that any area of your life is not Christian, that there is any area of your life about which you can say, "I won't decide." You must make decisions at every point, because Christianity says that our faith matters. In any area that you choose not to make a decision, you are telling us that your faith is irrelevant. We are called to do the Christian thing. It may be risky, but we must do it. One of my seminary professors, Dr. Ed Carnell, used to say, "There are four steps: Step number one, gather the facts; step number two, weigh them carefully; step number three, decide prayerfully; step number four, rest in your decision." Choose carefully and prayerfully, look at all the issues, make your decision as a believer, and rest in it, believing that God has you. I don't know what you are facing, but you need to bring the full impact of those facts in touch with your faith and be able to say, "This is the Christian thing to do, so help me, God!"

A recent issue of one of the airline magazines has an article called "Diogenes Is Looking for a Few Good Men."[3] "In an age of moral drift honesty proves an anchor for some, a ball and chain for others, and a dilemma in a world of business ethics." The article begins with the story of Richard Wooton, thirty-two years of age, who on a cool December afternoon in 1982 got off BART (the commuter train) in Concord, saw a package with no name or labeling on it. He was curious. There was no one around. He picked it up, opened it, and found that it was full of money. He counted out

$10,000, only a small part of what was in the package. He took it home, and counted the $40,000 to $50,000 that was in it. He wrestled with his decision for a few hours and then called a friend, and with that friend Wooton took the package to the police station.

The story became public news. Some said, "My, what a worthy man!" Others said, "He's crazy. He should have kept it." The article goes on to say that he was an alcoholic who had just become a born-again Christian whose life had been radically changed. In the light of that faith, he turned the package in.

Making decisions as a Christian ought to make a difference. "If the Son shall make you free, you shall be free indeed." When Jesus Christ comes into a man or woman's life, He gives them a new power, a new conviction, a new clarity. They become new men and new women in Christ Jesus, and it makes a difference. It ought to. When you bow your head and receive Christ into your life and become a new person, you become a person empowered by the Spirit of God and able to make decisions that please Him. So help us, God!

For Further Thought

1. What are some of the contemporary ideas that frustrate you regarding ethical decision making?

2. Are you tempted by situation ethics? Why do you think this is so?

3. What principles govern your life as a Christian decision maker?

4. What plans do you have to enable you to be more Christlike as you relate to your world?

Notes
1. Joseph Fletcher, *Situation Ethics* (Philadelphia: Westminster Press, 1966).
2. Charles Sheldon, *In His Steps* (Chicago: Advance Publishing Co., 1898).
3. Jay Stuller, "Diogenes Is Looking for a Few Good Men," *PSA*, May, 1983, p. 91.